STEPPING OUT

A JOURNEY THROUGH
BIBLICAL PROPHECY

July 13

STEPPING OUT

A JOURNEY THROUGH BIBLICAL PROPHECY

PAUL MCWHIRTER

FATHER'S HOUSE PRESS

CORNWALL, UK

First published in the UK in 2013 by
Father's House Press

Email: info@fathershousepress.com
Website: fathershousepress.com

ISBN: 978-0-957692206

Unless otherwise indicated, Scripture quotations are from the New King James Version of the Bible.

Cover image: Angela Jones Design

Printed and bound in the United Kingdom by
T J International Ltd, Padstow, Cornwall PL28 8RW

TO BILL

CONTENTS

ACKNOWLEDGEMENTS

First and foremost I would like to thank Elizabeth West for her wise insight, guidance and proof reading during the development stage of this project, without whose assistance a number of important issues would have been omitted from this book.

Second, I would like to thank Trystan Tragenza-Hall and Andrew Pilcher for their continued support and enthusiastic encouragement over the past few years as this book has developed.

Third, I would also like to thank Andrew and Ann Chapple for their vision for this project and for all their assistance in bringing 'Stepping Out' to publication.

Finally I would especially like to thank my fiancé Angela Jones for her ongoing faithful prayer support over the past five years and for the cover design which highlights the path we all need to travel - 'From Darkness To Light', to you, many many thanks.

Please note: The views expressed in this book are the views of the author and do not necessarily reflect the views of those who are mentioned above.

FOREWORD

My friend and I often sat in serious conversation beside the waterfront at Falmouth, Cornwall, UK. Our conversations usually centred upon God's plans for Israel and the return of Jesus. My friend's focus tended towards Israel and God's restoration of that special nation and my focus tended towards the end times and the return of Jesus.

As we talked one summer afternoon, the relationship between Israel and the return of Jesus became abundantly clear and with this conversation I came to fully understand God's ultimate plan for this world in which we live. The conversations we had during that year also helped with the planning of the final format of this book.

Finally, as this book has come to completion, I have been asked on numerous occasions, "Who has this book been written for?" All I can say is that this book 'STEPPING OUT' has been written for every person who has an interest and a concern for this world in which we live, *apologies for not being able to be more specific.*

With the above in mind, I have written this book in a

straight forward manner, giving a brief account of a very personal journey into the understanding of Biblical Prophecy.

This is not an academic book, nor is it intended to be a complete treatise on biblical prophecy and the end times. My only desire is that it would bless and encourage all who read.

Not everyone will agree with the conclusions I draw, but this has not been my prime objective. My prime objective and driving ambition is to enthuse all who desire to understand Biblical Prophecy and the return of Jesus, and encourage them to discover for themselves what the Bible has to say about this vitally important subject.

'STEPPING OUT' is the first in the series of four independent books titled, 'A JOURNEY THROUGH BIBLICAL PROPHECY',

Introduction

In Remembrance

I recorded the following thoughts shortly after the terrorist attack on the World Trade Centre in September 2001, these thoughts sum up the only hope we have for a world which has grown so much dimmer.

> This morning I finished reading through a newsletter produced by a well-respected Bible teacher and author. The newsletter discussed current major political, religious and environmental issues which could point to the soon return of Jesus. I make a note to follow up on some of the issues raised by the author.

> The time is now mid-morning and as I take a walk to a friend's house I reflect on the issues I have been reading. As we talk my friend tells me terrorists have just flown a plane into the World trade Centre in New York. I listen, yet I think her comments are some form of joke and I cannot believe what she is saying.

> My mind turns quickly back to the days when I

used to sail in and out of New York, Baltimore and Florida on ships loaded with fruit from Central America. First the Statue of Liberty and then the amazing Manhattan skyline with the twin towers of the World Trade Centre.

By mid afternoon I am sitting alone, numb, as I watch live news images project into my lounge. The news commentators would not be drawn into speculating on the number of possible casualties and deaths, except on one or two occasions the television broadcaster has the decency not to show people jumping from the skyscrapers.

As images of the planes crashing into the towers are continually repeated, I keep wondering how this atrocity will end. I am saddened knowing loved ones will be parted forever and saddened as more people enter eternity without knowing Jesus.

We may look at the darkness surrounding us and ask, Where is God? and wonder who will listen to His voice. The thoughts of terror are not God's thoughts, the way of terror is not God's way; terror is of the night and can in no way be justified. Thankfully our God does care for all that He created and without His goodness and grace there would be no hope for this world.

For now, I think of those who will lift their fist

and curse God, but I am also reminded of the soon return of Jesus and of the time of darkness that will come before that great and glorious day.

I pray this coming night will be short and the light of Jesus will shine in this very dark place.

There is no easy answer to the current political situation, and I hope and pray the raised fist will turn palm upwards and open and say, 'Return Lord Jesus, Return'.

TWELVE YEARS ON

Many world changing events have taken place since that day; there is continued disintegration of society and on-going political upheaval and wars that never seem to end. Along with many natural disasters there would appear to be no sign of the peace world leaders have continually promised. And for the first time in world history all this activity, along with new pandemic diseases, are taking place on a global scale. Is all that continues to take place not a strong reminder of the warning signs declared by Jesus regarding His soon return?

For now all who have ears to hear let them hear and take heed of the warning and promises given by our returning King.

Paul McWhirter

Chapter 1.

....

The Awakening

"Jesus returning to earth!" I exclaimed, "How can this be? Why have I not heard of this before? When will He return?" Little did I realise the disciples asked these very same questions of Jesus all those years ago.

One day before His crucifixion Jesus stood by the Temple in Jerusalem waiting for His disciples.

> *Matt 24 :1-3*
> *1 Then Jesus went out and departed from the temple, and His disciples came up to show Him the buildings of the temple.*
> *2 And Jesus said to them, "Do you not see all these things? Assuredly, I say to you, not one stone shall be left here upon another, that shall not be thrown down."*
> *3 Now as He sat on the Mount of Olives, the disciples came to Him privately, saying, "Tell us, when will these things be? And what will be the sign of Your coming, and of the end of the age?"*

In the discussion Jesus had with His Disciples He was

quite insistent with them that they should know and be aware of the Signs of the Times: He told them to be ever watchful and always ready and prepared for His return. Just as that message applied to those early disciples, so this same message applies ever more to us today.

WELCOME TO THE WORLD OF ESCHATOLOGY.

ES+CHA+TOL+O+GY: The branch of theology or biblical exegesis concerned with the end of the world. [from the Greek - *Eskhatos* - meaning last and - *logy* - meaning "the study of"].

BIBLE PROPHECY: Events recorded in the Bible that will take place at a future date: Often apocalyptic in nature.

A+POC+A+LYPSE: From the Greek: Apokalupsis, meaning - Appearing, Coming, Manifestation, Revelation. The events leading to the end of the world and the return of Jesus.

APOCALYPSE: General secular usage - any major catastrophic event, natural or man-made disasters, generally violent in nature.

THE SEARCH

My teenage imagination was fired up, I was intrigued with the prospect of the return of Jesus, 'How could I not get excited?' Those conversations Jesus had with His disciples conjured up images of strange beasts, earthquakes and wild storms. I was fascinated by this new world that had just opened up to me; this was a world full of unprecedented events and a world full of surprises greater than any adventure created by any human being.

But this adventure began many years earlier.

As far as I can remember I had always enjoyed discovering new aspects of the world around me, yet from a very young age religion had been a puzzle.

During my early teens I was particularly interested in natural history, geology, astronomy, arts & crafts, model making as well as all the usual things a growing boy got interested in. But my real longing was to find a sense of place in this world and I strongly desired to discover the reason and purpose for my existence, and through this sprang a conscious desire to find God.

In my junior years at school my teacher would read the story of Abraham, Isaac and Jacob to her class. Another teacher would encourage her class to memorise verses from the 'Sermon on the Mount'. One Easter the life of Jesus was presented as a modern day radio news broadcast, and this school radio production took me straight into the world of the Middle East. I could hear the noises in the busy streets, see the bartering in the market and even smell the grumpy camels. I wept with Mary and John as Jesus was being crucified, hoping against hope that Jesus would live and not die.

In those early days I did not appreciate the

significance of the death of Jesus on the cross or the passages of scripture I was required to memorise at school. Strangely, it was these passages that would one day form the basis of the search that would fill my life. Then when I entered high school, the subjects I loved filled my time; sadly, I began to look to the creation and forgot about the Creator.

THE PATH TO FAITH

It was 1972, I had arrived at a crossroads which appeared to have no clear signpost. I had reached my mid-teens and was very lost; I began to question my very existence. On entering college that year my interest in ecological issues sharpened and I became very concerned about the damage we were doing to the world around us, especially as we appeared to be destroying this beautiful planet.

Like many others, I was convinced time was running out for this world and the thought of a nuclear disaster, another ice age or the earth burning up in a third world war was never far from my mind. In those pre-oil crisis days, global warming, the thinning of the ozone layer and the destruction of the rain forests were problems only just being realised.

During this search I seriously began to look for a purpose and meaning to life, but the many books I read were not able to answer the big questions: How did the universe come into existence? Was there an ultimate intelligence behind the formation of the universe? Did God exist? I longed to know, but in finding no clear answer, my search continued.

THE MEETING

It was a cold, wet November evening, the place was South Shields at the mouth of the river Tyne in the North East of England. I stopped my motorcycle alongside a very startled clergyman who lived nearby. Although I had been noticing this clergyman for a number of weeks, this was my first encounter with Charles.

I was very suspicious of the Church and its preachers and I viewed Christianity as a hypocritical religion that bore no relationship to the world in which I lived; however, here was I being drawn to this stranger. We talked for a short time and made arrangements to meet. On our second encounter, I soon realised Charles had a strong faith yet he was prepared to listen to what I had to say. I attempted to turn Charles around to my way of thinking; but I was intrigued by his faith and beliefs: How could a man like Charles, with his intellectual background, believe the Bible and what it said?

To my astonishment Charles not only believed in a God who loved and cared for His creation, but he believed in a God who longed for His creation to come to Him. Charles also believed that Jesus would return to earth and establish His eternal kingdom. This was certainly not the cold and distant God I had been brought up to believe in. Furthermore, Charles believed that each person who searched for God with their whole heart would find Him, and eventually I became one of those who searched and found.

With this new faith, I had discovered what I had always been looking and longing for, and as my life turned in a new direction it took on new meaning and purpose. I could be confident in the knowledge that God loved me and wanted me for His very own.

Dorothy, a friend of Charles, now his wife, gave me a copy of the Bible to read and Charles continued to nurture my young faith and encouraged me to study. I soon read through all four Gospels and headed into the Book of Acts, I was transfixed - the Bible was truly alive. I later realised this was our loving heavenly Father drawing me to Himself, and it was He who brought the pages of the Bible to life.

CHAPTER 2.

....

THE END IN SIGHT

During those early years of my new found faith the return of Jesus and the prophetic implications of the re-establishment of Israel were being fervently discussed in many Christian circles. The book, 'The Late Great Planet Earth' had just been published and along with the apocalyptic film, 'A Thief in the Night', which included the Larry Norman song, 'I Wish We Had All Been Ready', were bringing many people to a faith in God. And so I turned to the Book of Revelation.

As I considered this last book of the Bible, I was amazed at what I read, 'How could any person understand such text?' 'How could anyone fathom such a fantastic story?' In my attempt to understand the visions God gave the Apostle John, I failed. Little did I realise an explanation of these visions was contained in the very Bible I held in my hands.

One major prophetic word I discovered in the Bible stated that Israel as a nation, (that is, the descendants of Abraham, Isaac and Jacob) would accept Jesus as Messiah, before He returned.

I soon learned that the first major step in this process, as believed by many followers of Jesus, was the establishment of the State of Israel as a fully fledged and independent nation with its own geographical borders being recognised and accepted by the United Nations.

Friends continually argued with me stating that this re-establishment of Israel had no bearing on the return of Jesus, but I was often reminded of the very words of Paul to the believers in Rome:-

> *Rom 11:25-27*
> *25 For I do not desire, brethren, that you should be ignorant of this mystery, lest you should be wise in your own opinion, that blindness in part has happened to Israel until the fullness of the Gentiles has come in.*
> *26 And so all Israel will be saved, as it is written: "The Deliverer will come out of Zion, And He will turn away ungodliness from Jacob;*
> *27 For this is My covenant with them, When I take away their sins".*

God continues to long for His people to come to Him and as He casts His gaze towards Israel, Israel is finally beginning to respond.

> *Matt 23:37-39*
> *37 "O Jerusalem, Jerusalem, the one who kills the prophets and stones those who are sent to her! How often I wanted to gather your children together, as a hen gathers her chicks under her wings, but you were not willing!*

38 See! Your house is left to you desolate;
39 for I say to you, you shall see Me no more till you
say, 'Blessed is He who comes in the name of the
Lord!'"

God states in His word that His love for His people of Israel is everlasting, and He will continue to have a special place in His heart for this very special nation, even unto the time of the return of Jesus.

As my journey continued, I yearned to have a greater understanding of the end times and the return of Jesus, yet my lack of knowledge of the Bible and Bible Prophecy proved to be extremely frustrating. I had reached a complete impasse and began to wonder if Jesus was really going to return as He said He would.

Was I now to go the way of my friends and reject the idea of a literal return of Jesus or would I continue on with my venture? As I pondered, I turned to the Book of Matthew and there lay the key to my search.

THE KEY - THE OLIVET DISCOURSE MATT 24 & LUKE 21

Towards the end of His life on earth, Jesus began to prepare the disciples for His departure. And there on the Mount of Olives Jesus sat talking with His followers on the very place where Zachariah records Messiah would place His feet when He came to earth.

This discussion Jesus had with His followers that day is recorded in Matthew chapter 24 and in Luke Chapter 21 and is often called the Olivet Discourse.

The first thirty-one verses of Matthew chapter 24 can

be broken into seven sections and can be seen as describing the past two thousand years of history:-

1 - THE DESTRUCTION OF THE TEMPLE

Matt 24:1-2
1 Then Jesus went out and departed from the temple, and His disciples came up to show Him the buildings of the temple.
2 And Jesus said to them, "Do you not see all these things? Assuredly, I say to you, not one stone shall be left here upon another, that shall not be thrown down."

The destruction of Herod's Temple in Jerusalem happened just as Jesus predicted. This event took place in 70 AD only six years after the Temple was completed. This was surely the first major prophetic warning of Jesus to be fulfilled.

2 - FALSE CHRISTS OR MESSIAHS

Matt 24:3-5
3 Now as He sat on the Mount of Olives, the disciples came to Him privately, saying, "Tell us, when will these things be? And what will be the sign of Your coming, and of the end of the age?"
4 And Jesus answered and said to them: "Take heed that no one deceives you.
5 For many will come in My name, saying, 'I am the Christ,' and will deceive many".

Paul often instructed the brethren to beware of wolves who would come in sheep's clothing and who would attempt to deceive many. And looking at today's cults and New Age movement, many of their leaders claim to be the Christ with many of their beliefs rooted within the Gnostic and pagan religions of the first and second centuries following the birth of Jesus.

3 - WARS AND RUMOURS OF WAR

Matt 24:6-8
6 "And you will hear of wars and rumours of wars. See that you are not troubled; for all these things must come to pass, but the end is not yet.
7 For nation will rise against nation, and kingdom against kingdom. And there will be famines, pestilences, and earthquakes in various places.
8 All these are the beginning of sorrows".

From the days of Jesus, warfare has continued to plague the nations.

During this past century alone, the carnage across Europe has been on an unprecedented scale. Following the end of the First World War more people died from disease, influenza and hunger than during the war itself.

Major earthquakes have continued throughout the world, and with the increase in world travel new pandemic diseases have also arisen - all foretold over two thousand years ago.

4 - TRIBULATION, BETRAYAL AND LAWLESSNESS

Matt 24:9-13
9 "Then they will deliver you up to tribulation and kill you, and you will be hated by all nations for My name's sake.
10 And then many will be offended, will betray one another, and will hate one another.

11 Then many false prophets will rise up and deceive many.
12 And because lawlessness will abound, the love of many will grow cold.
13 But he who endures to the end shall be saved".

Since the time of Jesus believers have been persecuted; however, in a time soon to come, every nation will turn against the Gospel message, and this on an unprecedented scale. In the coming days those who would claim to be prophets of God, and who are not, will continue to make every attempt to deceive the world and bring discredit upon the people of God. In this, many believers will lose heart but those who endure to the end will be saved.

5 - THE GOSPEL PROCLAIMED ACROSS THE WORLD

Matt 24:14
14 "And this gospel of the kingdom will be preached in all the world as a witness to all the nations, and then the end will come".

During past centuries the Gospel message has travelled around the earth, and although there are individuals and peoples who have not heard the Gospel message, every major division of humanity and language group have heard the truth about Jesus.

6 - THE ABOMINATION AND THE FLIGHT FROM JERUSALEM

Matt 24: 15-22
15 "Therefore when you see the 'abomination of desolation,' spoken of by Daniel the prophet, standing in the holy place" (whoever reads, let him understand),

16 "then let those who are in Judea flee to the mountains.
17 Let him who is on the housetop not go down to take anything out of his house.
18 And let him who is in the field not go back to get his clothes.
19 But woe to those who are pregnant and to those who are nursing babies in those days!
20 And pray that your flight may not be in winter or on the Sabbath.
21 For then there will be great tribulation, such as has not been since the beginning of the world until this time, no, nor ever shall be.
22 And unless those days were shortened, no flesh would be saved; but for the elect's sake those days will be shortened".

We are now confronted with some very specific prophetic words of Jesus which are a direct quote from the Book of Daniel. Jesus tells the disciples of an Abomination that will be raised up on the Temple Mount and when this coming time approaches, those living in Jerusalem and in the surrounding area will be required to flee to a place of safety provided by God.

Those who obey and flee will be kept safe, and there in the place provided by God, God will draw all Israel back fully to Himself. Then, when Jesus returns, God will bring this present age to a close.

7 - THE TIME OF THE END

Matt 24:23-31
23 "Then if anyone says to you, 'Look, here is the Christ!' or 'There!' do not believe it.
24 For false christs and false prophets will rise and show great signs and wonders to deceive, if possible,

even the elect.
25 See, I have told you beforehand.
26 Therefore if they say to you, 'Look, He is in the desert!' do not go out; or 'Look, He is in the inner rooms!' do not believe it.
27 For as the lightning comes from the east and flashes to the west, so also will the coming of the Son of Man be.
28 For wherever the carcass is, there the eagles will be gathered together.
29 Immediately after the tribulation of those days the sun will be darkened, and the moon will not give its light; the stars will fall from heaven, and the powers of the heavens will be shaken.
30 Then the sign of the Son of Man will appear in heaven, and then all the tribes of the earth will mourn, and they will see the Son of Man coming on the clouds of heaven with power and great glory.
31 And He will send His angels with a great sound of a trumpet, and they will gather together His elect from the four winds, from one end of heaven to the other".

Jesus now warns the disciples not to listen to rumours about His return, because His return will be for all to see: Then, according to the Book of Revelation, Jesus will reign on earth with the saints for a thousand years, and this in preparation for the establishment of God's eternal kingdom.

No person alive at this present time can fully comprehend what this return of Jesus will be like; however, following Jesus return we can be assured the world's order will be restored to God's order. In this coming time God will prove to the human race that His ways are faultless and true, and as stated by Isaiah (chapters 11 and 65), this coming time will be the time of true un-surpassing peace, a time of God's true Shalom upon the earth.

ETERNITY TO FOLLOW

For those who respond to God's call, who accept Jesus as Messiah and who carry out His word, can look forward to a new and eternal life with their loving creator God. In many respects, those who follow and have accepted Jesus have already entered eternity.

> *1 Cor 2:9*
> *9 But as it is written "Eye has not seen nor ear heard Nor have entered into the heart of man, the things which God has prepared for those who love Him.*

Our time throughout this coming eternity will not be a hazy time of floating around on clouds as many would have us believe. Our time throughout eternity will be both very physical and very spiritual, a time when God will allow us to explore the full mysteries of His new creation and universe.

This eternity will be an eternity of unrestricted access, creativity and of an ever growing love, knowledge and worship of God, and this with all that we are, with all that we do and all that we will become.

CHAPTER 3.

....

THE LIFE AND MESSAGE OF MESSIAH

THE COMING OF JESUS

For many a Jewish mother there has always been the desire to be the one who would give birth to that unique person, Messiah. This special person was to be known by such titles as:-

The Coming One, The Anointed One, One Set Apart For High Office, Emmanuel.

During times of great difficulty this promise of Messiah has been a great comfort to the people of Israel. According to the prophet Isaiah, this Messiah was to have a 'dual role', that of a suffering Servant and a conquering King.

With reference to Isaiah and to Hebraic tradition, this suffering servant has been known as Messiah ben Joseph, the son of Joseph, who would come in the spirit and suffering of Joseph; then there would be Messiah ben David, the son of David, who would come as a conquering King in the spirit of David and then rule and reign from a reconstructed Temple in Jerusalem. Little was it realised, Messiah ben Joseph, and Messiah ben David would be one of the same person, the Son of the living God.

Furthermore, Hebrew scriptures record that in due course God would also reveal Himself to the gentile world. In this, the gentile nations would then be able to enter God's Kingdom and fully partake in the richness of blessing God is going to pour out on all who obey and follow His Son.

> *Isa. 11:10*
> *10 "and in that day there shall be a Root of Jesse, Who shall stand as a banner to the People; For the Gentiles shall seek Him, And His resting place shall glorious".*
> *Isa. 42:1*
> *1 "Behold! My Servant whom I uphold, My Elect One in whom My soul delights! I have put My Spirit upon Him; He will bring forth justice to the Gentiles."*

MESSIAH

Traditional Jewish society expressed its relationship with God through family ties and her commitment to Torah and her Hebraic traditions and beliefs. In this, Jewish families were held together by close knit family ties with the eldest male of the each house acting as both the head of the house and as priest to the household.

Then at the centre of the Jewish community was the synagogue which was the central place for local worship and ceremonies.

At the time of Jesus, the Jewish nation yearned to be free from the yoke of Roman occupation. Israel was yearning for a deliverer, the promised Messiah, the one who would free her from her oppressors. But when Jesus came, He came to deal with an enemy much closer to home, the enemy within.

The Jewish community was divided in its belief towards this coming Messiah. There were the secular Greek-influenced Jews who wanted to be free from the restrictions of Torah and the Mosaic Law, the Zealots who desired a revolutionary solution to Israel's Roman occupation and the religious communities, such as the Essenes, who totally separated themselves from Jewish society in preparation for the coming of God's kingdom to earth.

But Jesus had come to the ordinary and the needy folk of Israel, and amongst these ordinary folk were two special people, Simeon and Anna; both Simeon and Anna being dedicated to serving God within the Temple in Jerusalem.

And there in the Temple Simeon and Anna waited patiently for Messiah, desiring to see the redemption of God come to His people Israel.

> *Luke 2:25-26*
> *25 And behold, there was a man in Jerusalem whose name was Simeon, and this man was just and devout, waiting for the Consolation of Israel, and the Holy Spirit was upon him.*

*26 And it had been revealed to him by the Holy Spirit
that he would not see death before he had seen the
Lord's Christ.*
*Both Simeon and Anna practised a true and living
faith and knew of the Messianic promise recorded in
the Scriptures, in this, they were prepared for the
coming of Messiah.*
Luke 2:34-37
*34 Then Simeon blessed them, and said to Mary His
mother, "Behold, this Child is destined for the fall and
rising of many in Israel, and for a sign which will be
spoken against*
*35 (yes, a sword will pierce through your own soul
also), that the thoughts of many hearts may be
revealed."*
*36 Now there was one, Anna, a prophetess, the
daughter of Phanuel, of the tribe of Asher. She was of
a great age, and had lived with a husband seven
years from her virginity;*
*37 and this woman was a widow of about eighty-four
years, who did not depart from the temple, but served
God with fastings and prayers night and day.*

Following the birth of Jesus, Mary and Joseph brought
the babe to the Temple in Jerusalem to be dedicated,
there they marvelled at what they saw and heard.

On seeing Mary, Joseph and the babe, Anna
immediately rejoiced.

Luke 2:38-40
*38 And coming in that instant she gave thanks to the
Lord, and spoke of Him to all those who looked for
redemption in Jerusalem.*
*39 So when they had performed all things according
to the law of the Lord, they returned to Galilee, to
their own city, Nazareth.*
*40 And the Child grew and became strong in spirit,
filled with wisdom; and the grace of God was upon*

Him.

Not since the days of Moses and the prophets had the Jewish nation been so confronted by their God.

THE YOUNG JESUS

Scripture does not tell us much about the upbringing of Jesus except for one very telling occasion when, at the age of twelve, Jesus was taken by His parents to Jerusalem for Passover.

> *Luke 2:43-52*
> *42 And when He was twelve years old, they went up to Jerusalem according to the custom of the feast.*
> *43 When they had finished the days, as they returned, the Boy Jesus lingered behind in Jerusalem. And Joseph and His mother did not know it;*
> *44 but supposing Him to have been in the company, they went a day's journey, and sought Him among their relatives and acquaintances.*
> *45 So when they did not find Him, they returned to Jerusalem, seeking Him.*
> *46 Now so it was that after three days they found Him in the temple, sitting in the midst of the teachers, both listening to them and asking them questions.*
> *47 And all who heard Him were astonished at His understanding and answers.*
> *48 So when they saw Him, they were amazed; and His mother said to Him, "Son, why have You done this to us? Look, Your father and I have sought You anxiously."*
> *49 And He said to them, "Why did you seek Me? Did you not know that I must be about My Father's business?"*
> *50 But they did not understand the statement which He spoke to them.*
> *51 Then He went down with them and came to*

Nazareth, and was subject to them, but His mother
kept all these things in her heart.
52 And Jesus increased in wisdom and stature, and in
favour with God and men.

During their return journey home from Jerusalem, Mary and Joseph realised Jesus was missing from their company and so they returned to the city and there they found their son. For sitting in the Temple in Jerusalem, in discussion with the religious teachers, was Jesus. Even at such a young age Jesus was able to discuss the many questions put to Him, causing all, including his parents, to look on in amazement.

According to Luke, on that particular year when Jesus was brought to Jerusalem He was twelve years of age. And yet when we look closely at this passage of scripture, it would suggest that during this Passover feast Jesus may have turned thirteen; this being the age at which a Jewish male-child is recognised and accepted as a man. This would also explain why Jesus was able to sit amongst the teachers of the Law, and on this occasion, the teachers would have heard Jesus read Torah in public or the first time.

Through Jesus ability to sit and discuss matters of the Mosaic Law and Scripture, it is very clear that Mary and Joseph had been faithful in their calling to bring Jesus up in the ways of God and in accordance with the will and purposes of God. With this upbringing, the path Jesus would take in later life was well prepared. It is also interesting to note that the teaching and ministry of Jesus is totally and completely rooted in His Hebraic heritage, tradition and upbringing.

Furthermore, Jesus' life was a complete fulfilment of the prophetic message contained within Hebrew Scriptures, and there is not one aspect of the teaching of Jesus that would suggest He ever travelled beyond the borders of Israel or travelled to study under some Guru in a foreign land as many New Age thinkers believe.

THE BAPTISM AND TEMPTATION OF JESUS

Before Jesus stepped out to declare God's message to the people of Israel, John the Baptist came first to prepare the way of Messiah.

> *Matt 3:1-3*
> *1 In those days John the Baptist came preaching in the wilderness of Judea,*
> *2 and saying, "Repent, for the kingdom of heaven is at hand!"*
> *3 For this is he who was spoken of by the prophet Isaiah, saying: "The voice of one crying in the wilderness: 'Prepare the way of the LORD; Make His paths straight.'"*

John has often been called the last of the Old Testament prophets, he was the last in respect of preaching the need to repent and prepare for the coming of Messiah; then with the coming of Jesus, John's message changed accordingly.

Matt 3:11
*"I indeed baptise you with water unto repentance but
He who is coming after me is mightier than I whose
sandals I am not worthy to carry He will baptise you
with the Holy Spirit and fire".*

John had a very clear understand of the nature of God
and the effect God's intervention in the affairs of Man
would have. Then with the coming of Jesus, John's
message was coming to an end.

Matt 3:14-17
*14 And John tried to prevent Him, saying, "I need to
be baptized by You, and are You coming to me?"*
*15 But Jesus answered and said to him, "Permit it to
be so now, for thus it is fitting for us to fulfil all
righteousness." Then he allowed Him.*
*16 When He had been baptized, Jesus came up
immediately from the water; and behold, the heavens
were opened to Him, and He saw the Spirit of God
descending like a dove and alighting upon Him.*
*17 And suddenly a voice came from heaven, saying,
"This is My beloved Son, in whom I am well pleased."*

Following His baptism, Jesus was led by the Holy Spirit
into the wilderness to fast and pray for forty days and
nights in preparation for His ministry upon the earth.
Towards the end of this time of fasting Satan tempted
Jesus and questioned His very identity.

Matt 4:3-10
*3 Now when the tempter came to Him, he said, "If
You are the Son of God, command that these stones
become bread."*
*4 But He answered and said, "It is written, 'Man shall
not live by bread alone, but by every word that
proceeds from the mouth of God.'"*
5 Then the devil took Him up into the holy city, set

Him on the pinnacle of the temple,
6 and said to Him, "If You are the Son of God, throw
Yourself down. For it is written: 'He shall give His
angels charge over you,' and, 'In their hands they
shall bear you up, Lest you dash your foot against a
stone.'"
7 Jesus said to him, "It is written again, 'You shall not
tempt the Lord your God.'"
8 Again, the devil took Him up on an exceedingly high
mountain, and showed Him all the kingdoms of the
world and their glory.
9 And he said to Him, "All these things I will give You
if You will fall down and worship me."
10 Then Jesus said to him, "Away with you, Satan!
For it is written, 'You shall worship the Lord your God,
and Him only you shall serve.'"

Jesus was secure in His relationship with His heavenly Father; Jesus knew exactly who He was and the calling His Father had placed upon His life. And during this time of fasting, Jesus never wavered, for He knew that Satan's offer would divert Him completely from God's plan of salvation for His creation. God had only one plan of deliverance and that is through His Son, Jesus of Nazareth.

With Satan's failure to direct Jesus away from His heavenly Father, God's angels came and ministered to Him. And from this place of victory Jesus returned to Galilee in the power and strength of God's Holy Spirit.

Following this encounter with Jesus, Satan continued to pursue Him and attempted to snare Him at every opportunity and have Him arrested and killed before His time.

JESUS AND HIS PUBLIC MINISTRY

On return to Nazareth and as was His custom, Jesus went into the synagogue on the Sabbath day (Saturday) and stood up to read. Jesus was handed the scroll of the prophet Isaiah and when He opened the scroll He found the place where it was written:

> *Luke 4:18-21*
> *18 "The Spirit of the Lord is upon Me, Because He has anointed Me To preach the gospel to the poor; He has sent Me to heal the broken hearted, To proclaim liberty to the captives And recovery of sight to the blind, To set at liberty those who are oppressed;*
> *19 To proclaim the acceptable year of the Lord."*

Through this particular reading, Jesus publicly stated, for the first time, that He came from God. By this declaration Jesus was letting the people of Nazareth know that He was the 'One', the long expected Messiah. And news of Him spread quickly throughout the region.

> *20 Then He closed the book, and gave it back to the attendant and sat down. And the eyes of all who were in the synagogue were fixed on Him.*
> *21 And He began to say to them, "Today this Scripture is fulfilled in your hearing.*

The people of Nazareth knew the scripture from which Jesus read. On quoting from the Book of Isaiah Jesus took upon Himself the responsibility of that prophetic word and the consequence of such a declaration.

There was no doubt, no ambiguity, Jesus declared Himself to be the chosen one, God's Saviour and coming King, Messiah.

THE DEATH OF JOHN THE BAPTIST

During these early days of Jesus ministry, John the Baptist had been put in prison for criticising Herod. Then when Jesus heard of this He went to dwell in Capernaum which is by the Sea of Galilee.

While there by the sea, Jesus called His disciples and also began to declare, "Repent, for the kingdom of Heaven is at hand."   And there in the region of Zebulon and Naphtali God's prophetic word was fulfilled.

While John was in prison, John sent his disciples to enquire of Jesus.

Matt 11:2-6
2 And when John had heard in prison about the works of Christ, he sent two of his disciples
3 and said to Him, "Are You the Coming One, or do we look for another?"
4 Jesus answered and said to them, "Go and tell John the things which you hear and see:
5 The blind see and the lame walk; the lepers are cleansed and the deaf hear; the dead are raised up and the poor have the gospel preached to them.
6 And blessed is he who is not offended because of Me."

With this passage being a direct quote from the Book of Isaiah, Jesus again confirmed His identity.

Isa 35:5-6
5 Then the eyes of the blind shall be opened, And the ears of the deaf shall be unstopped.

6 Then the lame shall leap like a deer, And the tongue of the dumb sing. For waters shall burst forth in the wilderness, And streams in the desert.

Please note: With Jesus omitting to quote Isaiah 35 verse 4, this would suggest that Jesus was gently indicating to John that John would not get out of prison a free man.

Isa 35:4
Say to those who are fearful-hearted, "Be strong, do not fear! Behold your God will come with vengeance, With the recompense of God; He will come and save you."

Jesus directed John's disciples to look and see for themselves what was happening and then report back to John. John would understand the significance of the miracles Jesus performed, the miracles pointing to Jesus being the Anointed One - Messiah.

Then with the beheading of John, John's earlier declaration in John Ch. 3:30 *"He must increase, and I must decease"* came to its ultimate conclusion.

THE SERMON ON THE MOUNT AND THE KINGDOM OF GOD

Early in Jesus ministry, Jesus revealed His full plan and intention through the proclamation of His manifesto, often called the 'Sermon on the Mount' (Matthew, Ch 5 to 7). In this, Jesus declared the way of discipleship and set in place the principles by which every believer would be required to live.

These principles were revolutionary and would be able

to cross all national and cultural boundaries and even transcend over two thousand years of history, up to this present day.

As part of this life in God Kingdom, God has placed into our hands a great and grave responsibility, the Great Commission (Matthew 28:16-20), and in this, the eternal souls of every person living on planet earth.

THE COVENANT AND THE KINGDOM

At the heart of God's new Kingdom was a new Law which came with a new set of values, and these values were to be placed within the very being of all who accepted Jesus and the message He brought.

In this, God's kingdom was to be like no other:

> *Rom 14:17*
> *"Do For the kingdom of God is not eating and drinking but righteousness and peace and joy in the Holy Spirit.*

Through this message, Jesus revealed the Law of the Kingdom, and all who accept this Law take the first step towards life in God's new kingdom. This new Law was not intended to replace the Law of Moses, but to fulfil it and bring it to its fullest expression.

> *Matt 5:17*
> *"Do not think that I came to destroy the Law or the Prophets. I did not come to destroy but to fulfil."*

This new Law brought in its way a new way of living and this was to be far more rigorous and demanding than the Law God gave to Moses. Yet despite its demands this new Law of the kingdom had one distinct advantage; living within this Law would not be worked out with a person's own strength or ability, but by God through the power of God's Holy Spirit at work in every individual believer.

> *Gal 2:20*
> *"I have been crucified with Christ; it is no longer I who live, but Christ lives in me; and the life which I now live in the flesh I live by faith in the Son of God, who loved me and gave Himself for me. "*

With this new Law the foundation upon which God would build His eternal kingdom was now established.

JEREMIAH AND THE NEW COVENANT

> *Jer 31:31-33*
> *31 "Behold, the days are coming, says the Lord, when I will make a new covenant with the house of Israel and with the house of Judah*
> *32 not according to the covenant that I made with their fathers in the day that I took them by the hand to lead them out of the land of Egypt, My covenant which they broke, though I was a husband to them, says the Lord.*
> *33 But this is the covenant that I will make with the house of Israel after those days, says the Lord: I will put My law in their minds, and write it on their hearts; and I will be their God, and they shall be My people".*

God's new Law was to centre upon the New Covenant as declared through the prophet, Jeremiah. This was a promise first given to Israel and is at the heart of God's plan for His coming Kingdom on earth.

This new kingdom was not just intended to be a

spiritual kingdom but it was intended to be both practical as well as spiritual. This new kingdom was intended to permeate every aspect of a person's being; how they relate to God, how they treat their neighbour and themselves, their livestock, possessions and the environment in which they live.

Ultimately this New Covenant was intended to be the seal by which every true believer is able to live a completely new and victorious way of life.

HALAKHAH

This new way of living, as commanded by Jesus, has strong similarities to the traditional Jewish Halakhah, that is, the Hebraic way of life.

> *HALAKHAH: Derived from the Hebrew word calash, meaning "going" or the "correct way", thus the literal translation, "the way to go".*

And so it is with Jesus, for He is our Halakhah, our way, our truth and our life, and in Him we find a new way of living and walking, and this by the light that Jesus shines forth from within every true believer.

> *Gal 2:20*
> *20 "I have been crucified with Christ; it is no longer I who live, but Christ lives in me; and the life which I now live in the flesh I live by faith in the Son of God, who loved me and gave Himself for me."*

Finally, to claim to live in and belong to the Kingdom of God and not fulfil the commands of Jesus, brings into question our very relationship with God and His Son

Jesus our Messiah.

THE PARABLES OF THE KINGDOM

The Parables of Jesus actually explore the relationship between God and His people and are intended to give understanding to the nature of God's kingdom upon the earth.

Initially, the teachings of Jesus were clear for all to hear and understand, but sadly there came a time when the words of Jesus were being rejected by those who would not listen.

And this was the time when Jesus began to speak in parables.

> *Matt 13:10-13*
> *10 And the disciples came and said to Him, "Why do You speak to them in parables?"*
> *11 He answered and said to them, "Because it has been given to you to know the mysteries of the kingdom of heaven, but to them it has not been given.*
> *12 For whoever has, to him more will be given, and he will have abundance; but whoever does not have, even what he has will be taken away from him.*
> *13 Therefore I speak to them in parables, because seeing they do not see, and hearing they do not hear, nor do they understand.*

These Parables are not merely moral tales, but they are at the heart of our relationship with God. They link the mortal with the immortal God, the finite with the infinite God and they are the very principles by which God is building His kingdom upon the earth.

But for those who reject these words of Jesus, they harden their own hearts to such an extent, God then prevents them from understanding His words.

The Parables recorded in Chapter 13 of the Book of Matthew can be divided into two groups:

THE FIRST GROUP OF PARABLES - Sowing and Growing - The Establishment of God's Kingdom on Earth and the First Coming of Jesus:

The Parable of the sower (v 3-9)

The Parable of the wheat and the tares (v 24-30)

The Parable of the mustard seed (v 32)

The Parable of the yeast (v 33-34)

This first group of parables relate to God sowing the seeds of faith and describes the kingdom of God as God intended. These parables are also the guide by which we can assess and measure the extent we allow God to work and penetrate our very being.

THE SECOND GROUP OF PARABLES - THE HARVEST OF THE KINGDOM - FINDING AND KEEPING AND THE RETURN OF JESUS:

The Parable of the Treasure (v 44)

The Parable of the Pearl (v 45-46)

The Parable of the Fishing Net (v 47-50)

The Parable of the Householder (v 52)

This second group of parables relate to the ultimate harvest at the end of the age, and yet they also speak of the individual believer's commitment to God and His kingdom in their day to day lives. With these Parables we gain a clearer understanding of the nature of God's kingdom, and as such, how much more should we take note of these treasures for which Jesus gave His life?

THE DEATH AND RESURRECTION OF JESUS: THE LAW AND PASSOVER

Throughout the Hebrew Bible, the Hebraic feasts can be seen to prophetically reflect the life and mission of Jesus.

> *Exo 12 :25-27*
> *25 It will come to pass when you come to the land which the Lord will give you, just as He promised, that you shall keep this service.*
> *26 And it shall be, when your children say to you, 'What do you mean by this service?'*
> *27 that you shall say, 'It is the Passover sacrifice of the Lord, who passed over the houses of the children of Israel in Egypt when He struck the Egyptians and delivered our households.'" So the people bowed their heads and worshiped.*

With the death of Jesus taking place at Passover and with Passover and the eating of the Passover Seder being a reminder to the Hebrew people of their freedom from slavery in Egypt; Passover can also be seen as a prophetic reminder of the death of Jesus and freedom He brought from eternal slavery.

> *Heb 8:4-5*
> *4 For if He were on earth, He would not be a priest,*

since there are priests who offer the gifts according to the law;
5 who serve the copy and shadow of the heavenly things, as Moses was divinely instructed when he was about to make the tabernacle. For He said, "See that you make all things according to the pattern shown you on the mountain."

WORDS FROM THE CROSS

The full significance of Jesus' declarations from the cross also reflect the true nature of God's kingdom on earth.

In total there were seven statements recorded in the Gospels which Jesus uttered and each statement has a significant place within the establishment of God's kingdom at the end of the age.

With Jesus first declaration from the cross, "Father, forgive them, for they do not know what they do." (Luke 23:34), Jesus reveals only true forgiveness comes from God and there is no other we can call on for our salvation.

Jesus second declaration from the cross, reveals the thief calling on forgiveness for his sin and Jesus declaring that he would be with Him in paradise that very day (Luke 23:43). With God's forgiveness we can truly be comforted knowing one day we too will be with Jesus for all eternity.

Jesus third declaration from the cross, "Woman, behold your son. Behold your mother" (John 19:26–27). Reflects the true caring side of God's nature and the need for us to comfort those who mourn. What greater example of God's love can be shown when Jesus lays aside His anguish and pain to care for the woman who supported and stood by Him from the days before His birth to the day of such a cruel death.

Jesus fourth declaration from the cross, "My God, My God, why have you forsaken me?" (Matthew 27:46). Jesus did not deserve to die, but died in our place and as the darkest night of His life approached He was separated from God for the first time in His entire existence. On the cross Jesus clothed Himself with the whole world's sin, He literally became sin for our sakes and took the punishment for all our wrong doing so we could walk in fellowship with His Father.

Jesus fifth declaration from the cross, "I am thirsty" (John 19:28). Of all the statements Jesus declared reminds us of so many of the aspects of the ministry of Jesus, from the Sermon on the Mount, to those He called who were thirsty and Jesus declaring to the woman at the well that He was the source of all living water.

Jesus sixth declaration from the cross, "It is finished" John 19:30. With the death of Jesus there was nothing else to be done to bring salvation to His creation. The work of Jesus was finished and His death brought an end to separation from God, all are now free to come and drink of God's goodness.

Jesus seventh and final declaration from the cross, "Father, into your hands I commit my spirit." Luke 23:46. Even in death and separation Jesus continued to trust in His loving heavenly Father and He knows His spirit will be safe in His Father's arms. In our walk with Jesus there is a continual need for us to trust our loving heavenly Father and as Jesus declared, part of our life in the Spirit is committing our lives and our ways continually into God's hands.

These seven declarations can be seen to sum up the nature of God's eternal kingdom and through this we too should be able to trust our loving heavenly Father to bring us to the place where we will be with Him for all eternity.

THE ANOMALY

There is no question as to the identity of Jesus and the authenticity of His death and resurrection, but there is an anomaly which has proved to be a stumbling block for many people, especially for those who come from a Jewish or Middle Eastern background and who, for good reason, find it difficult to consider or accept Jesus as Messiah.

If this anomaly was resolved, a greater understanding of the relationship between the prophetic fulfilment of Hebrew Scriptures and the life of Jesus and His return can be obtained.

TRADITIONAL GENTILE CHRISTIAN BELIEF

Before discussing the crucifixion and resurrection of Jesus, there is a need to consider two issues which affect how the timing of Jesus crucifixion and resurrection is understood.

First, unlike the western day that begins and finishes at midnight, the Jewish day begins at sundown one day and ends at sundown on the following day.

Second, there is a need to consider the relationship between the Jewish weekly Shabbat and the annual Passover Shabbat. The Jewish weekly Shabbat begins on Friday at sundown and ends Saturday sundown, this being fixed to the day of the week. The annual Passover Shabbat falls on the 15th of Nisan, being fixed to the day of the month, beginning at sundown and ending at sundown the following day.

This issue may seem a little irrelevant to the study of Biblical Prophecy, but in reality, the issues related to the timing of the death and resurrection of Jesus lie at the heart of the ability of bible prophecy to be interpreted in a literal manner.

Traditional gentile Christian belief states that Jesus was crucified on a Friday, on the day of preparation of the weekly Jewish Shabbat.

From a gentile Christian perspective, Jesus was crucified on Friday, the day of preparation of the weekly Shabbat, then He was taken down from the cross and place in the tomb late Friday afternoon, just before the Jewish weekly Shabbat began. Jesus is believed to have then risen from the dead early on Sunday morning, this being the first day of the week, just before the women came to prepare His body for final burial.

Following, is an outline of the traditional gentile Christian understanding of the time Jesus spent in the grave:-

Friday sunset to Saturday sunrise	12 hours
Saturday sunrise to Saturday sunset	12 hours
Saturday sunset to Sunday sunrise	<u>12 hours</u>
Time in the grave	36 hours

According to the above table, the total time Jesus would have been in the grave is 36 hours, which equals only one day and two nights, not quite the 72 hours that make up three full days and three full nights.

According to an Hebraic understanding of the timing of Jesus crucifixion, death, burial and resurrection, Jesus would have been crucified on the day of preparation of the annual Passover Shabbat, that is, the 14th of Nisan, rather than on the day of preparation of the weekly Shabbat. With this understanding, it would be then possible for Jesus to be in the grave for three full days and three full nights as required by scripture and the prophetic imagery of Jonah.

The Gospel of Matthew records Jesus telling the Scribes and the Pharisees that Jonah, being swallowed by a great fish, was a prophetic witness to His death and resurrection.

> *Mat 12:38-40*
> *38 Then some of the scribes and Pharisees answered, saying, "Teacher, we want to see a sign from You."*
> *39 But He answered and said to them, "An evil and adulterous generation seeks after a sign, and no sign will be given to it except the sign of the prophet Jonah.*
> *40 For as Jonah was three days and three nights in the belly of the great fish, so will the Son of Man be three days and three nights in the heart of the earth.*

Jesus then declared to the scribes and the Pharisees that He, the Son of Man, would be in the heart of the earth for that same period of time, three days and three nights, as Jonah was in the belly of the great fish.

> *Jonah 1:17*
> *17 Now the LORD had prepared a great fish to swallow Jonah. And Jonah was in the belly of the fish three days and three nights.*

Using the prophet Jonah as an example, Jesus confirmed the time span between His own death and His resurrection to be three days and three nights. Therefore, how can this anomaly be resolved? Thankfully a solution is at hand.

PASSOVER AND THE ANOMALY

With the death and resurrection of Jesus taking place at Passover, Jesus partook of the Passover Seder with His disciples at sundown at the beginning of the first day of Passover (14th of Nisan), this being the day of preparation for the Passover Shabbat which begins on the 15th of Nisan. This annual Passover Shabbat was to be a holy convocation where no laborious work was to be done.

Later on the same evening, after the Seder had been eaten and with Judas betraying Jesus, Jesus went out with His disciples to Gethsemane to pray through the night.

While there in Gethsemane, very early in the morning, Jesus was taken captive by the Roman guards to stand trial before Pilate.

By 9am that same day Jesus was crucified, He was then pronounced dead six hours later at 3pm (still on the 14th of Nisan).

That same day, immediately before the beginning of the annual Passover Shabbat (15th of Nisan), which began at sundown, Joseph of Arimathea took the body of Jesus down from the cross and placed it in his own unused tomb.

> *Luke 23:54-56*
> *54 That day was the Preparation, and the Sabbath drew near.*
> *55 And the women who had come with Him from Galilee followed after, and they observed the tomb*

and how His body was laid. 56 Then they returned and prepared spices and fragrant oils. And they rested on the Sabbath according to the commandment.

If on the year Jesus died, the annual Passover Seder was served on Tuesday evening at sundown, this being on the 14th of Nisan, Jesus would then have been crucified the following morning, Wednesday morning, still on the 14th of Nisan, the day of preparation of the annual Passover Shabbat.   The annual Passover Shabbat would then have begun at sundown that same day, the 15th of Nisan, and then finished the following day, Thursday, at sundown.

John 19:31
31 Therefore because it was the Preparation Day, and the bodies should not remain on the cross on the Sabbath, the Jews asked Pilate that their legs might be broken and that they might be taken away.

Therefore, according to this time scale, there would have been ample time for Jesus to be in the grave for three complete days and three complete nights (72 hours) and then rise again on the first day of the week.

Jesus could have risen as early as sundown on Saturday evening, with evening being the beginning of the following day within Jewish culture.

Time scale showing the hours related to the death of Jesus and time He spent in the grave:-

Wednesday sunset to Thursday sunrise (12 hours)

Thursday sunrise to Thursday sunset   (12 hours)

Thursday sunset to Friday sunrise   (12 hours)

Friday sunrise to Friday sunset   (12 hours)

Friday sunset to Saturday sunrise   (12 hours)

Saturday sunrise to Saturday sunset   <u>(12 hours)</u>

           Total time in the grave   (72 hours)

What clearer example can there be of Jesus being the ultimate prophetic fulfilment of the death of the Passover lamb than dying on the very day Passover was being observed?

If the above timing for a Wednesday crucifixion were adopted by the Church, this would add credible weight to the Gospel message and potentially cause the Church's attitude towards the Hebraic foundation of the Christian faith to be considered in a more favourable light.

With this, there would also be a need for the Church to re-evaluate its relationship to the Jewish festivals and especially the Christian celebration of Easter.

And for the true believer, Passover is a strong biblical reminder to us of the death and resurrection of Jesus, and of the hope that comes in its wake.

IN FAVOUR OF A WEDNESDAY CRUCIFIXION

There have been many noted believers in a

Wednesday crucifixion, early believers include Epiphanus, Vidorinus of Petua, Ladanius, Cassiodorius and Gregory of Tours then later, Wescott, Finis Dake and R. A. Torrey also recognised the possibility of a Wednesday crucifixion.

THE EARLY CHRISTIANS AND PASSOVER

The early church continued to celebrate Passover but in due course Passover lost its significance. The demise of the celebration of Passover was also exacerbated when the Bishops of Rome forbade Christians from taking part in the Passover meal. Those who partook were threatened with excommunication from the Church.

Further change came to pass when the Sabbath day was changed from Saturday to Sunday. This change was instituted by Sixus, the Bishop of Rome, just before the death of the Apostle John while John was in exile on the Isle of Patmos.

Later Bishops of Rome continued with this practice, but despite the differing arguments there was no biblical basis or justification for such a change. This action further alienated the community of believers from the Hebraic foundations and heritage of their faith.

RESURRECTION AND THE ROAD TO EMMAUS

Following the resurrection of Jesus as recorded in the Gospel according to Luke, Jesus revealed Himself to two of His disciples on the road leading to Emmaus.

Jesus explained to the two disciples all matters in scripture (the Old Testament) relate to Himself, beginning with Moses and the Prophets.

> *Luke 24 (Summary)   Two of the disciples of Jesus were travelling to a village called Emmaus which was approximately seven mites from Jerusalem. As they walked together they talked of the death of Jesus. While they conversed and reasons Jesus drew Himself near but they did not recognise Him. Jesus said to them, "What kind of conversation is this that you have with each other as you walk and are sad?"*
>
> *Then one of the disciples, named Cleopas, unknowingly described to Jesus how all their aspirations were based upon this one man they believed to be Messiah. Jesus then replied to the two disciples, "O foolish ones and slow of heart to believe in all that the prophets have spoken! Ought not the Christ to have suffered these things and to enter into His glory?" Beginning with Moses and the Prophets, Jesus expounded to them in all the scriptures the things concerning Himself.*
>
> *As they drew near to the village where they were going Jesus indicated that He would have to go further. But they constrained Him, saying, "Abide with us, for it is toward evening, and the day is far spent." And He went in to stay with them. Now it came to pass, as He sat at the table with them, that He took bread, bless and broke it, and gave it to them. Then their eyes were open and they knew Him and then He vanished from their sight. And they said to one another   "Did not our heart burn within us while He talked on the road, and while He opened the Scriptures to us?"*

Here in the Gospel of Luke, Jesus confirmed that He was the fulfilment of all Scripture, which makes up the Hebrew Bible, and Jesus continually referred back to the Hebrew text to confirm and establish His identity. In this, Messiah Jesus is totally inseparable from the Word of God given to the children of Abraham, Isaac and Jacob.

And finally, let us not forget:-

"O foolish ones, and slow of heart to believe in all that the prophets have spoken! Ought not the Christ to have suffered these things and to enter into His glory?"

And beginning with Moses and all the Prophets Jesus expounded to them from the Hebrew Scriptures all that concerned Himself

CHAPTER 4.

....

THE WAY AND THE KINGDOM

THE FOUNDING OF THE COMMUNITY OF BELIEVERS

Fifty days following Passover and the death and resurrection of Jesus we arrive at the heady day of Pentecost, otherwise known as Shavuot.

SHAVUOT: *The Feast of Weeks or the Feast of First Fruits; Shavuot, primarily an agricultural festival celebrating the gathering in of the grain harvest. Also commemorating the day on which God gave the Ten Commandments and the Law to Moses on Mt Sinai.*

PENTECOST: *from the Greek, meaning fiftieth, that is - fifty days after Passover.*

According to the Book of Leviticus, God instructed the Children of Israel to count forty nine days from the day after Passover on to the barley harvest. This barley harvest was then to be offered as a wave offering before the Lord, 'unto the day of Shavuot', with the wheat offering to follow.

> *Leviticus 23:15-17*
> *15 'And you shall count for yourselves from the day after the Sabbath (Passover), from the day that you brought the sheaf of the wave offering: seven Sabbaths shall be completed.*
> *16 Count fifty days to the day after the seventh Sabbath; then you shall offer a new grain offering to the Lord.*
> *17 You shall bring from your dwellings two wave loaves of two-tenths of an ephah. They shall be of fine flour; they shall be baked with leaven. They are the firstfruits to the Lord.*

By the giving the Ten Commandments and the Law to Moses at Mt Sinai, God set His Law and His Ordinances in place, these were the boundaries by which Israel was expected to live and flourish. And with this, the nation of Israel was formally established.

On this same day many centuries later, instead of God giving an outward Law, God gave the one hundred and twenty disciples an inward Law by filling them with His Holy Spirit. In this, God had sent His Holy Spirit to live and dwell in the very heart of those who would receive Him. And on this day in Jerusalem, the 'Church', with its inward spiritual Law was born, and with this, the greatest revolution this world has ever witnessed broke forth.

> *Acts 2:1*
> *1 When the Day of Pentecost had fully come, they were all with one accord in one place.*
> *2 And suddenly there came a sound from heaven, as of a rushing mighty wind, and it filled the whole*

house where they were sitting.
3 Then there appeared to them divided tongues, as of
fire, and one *sat upon each of them.*
4 And they were all filled with the Holy Spirit and
began to speak with other tongues, as the Spirit gave
them utterance.

With this outpouring of God's Holy Spirit, the ultimate expression of God's Law was manifest upon this gathering of one hundred and twenty disciples.

Acts 2:5-13
5 And there were dwelling in Jerusalem Jews, devout
men, from every nation under heaven.
6 And when this sound occurred, the multitude came
together, and were confused, because everyone
heard them speak in his own language.
7 Then they were all amazed and marvelled, saying to
one another, "Look, are not all these who speak
Galileans?
8 And how is it that we hear, each in our own
language in which we were born?
9 Parthians and Medes and Elamites, those dwelling in
Mesopotamia, Judea and Cappadocia, Pontus and
Asia,
10 Phrygia and Pamphylia, Egypt and the parts of
Libya adjoining Cyrene, visitors from Rome, both Jews
and proselytes,
11 Cretans and Arabs—we hear them speaking in our
own tongues the wonderful works of God."
12 So they were all amazed and perplexed, saying to
one another, "Whatever could this mean?"
13 Others mocking said, "They are full of new wine."

According to the Book of Acts, when God poured out His Holy Spirit, there were many Jews and gentile proselytes gathering in the city. These folk had come from all over the known world to celebrate the feast of

Shavuot.

> *Exodus 14-17*
> *14 "Three times you shall keep a feast to Me in the year:*
> *15 You shall keep the Feast of Unleavened Bread (you shall eat unleavened bread seven days, as I commanded you, at the time appointed in the month of Abib, for in it you came out of Egypt; none shall appear before Me empty);*
> *16 and the Feast of Harvest, the firstfruits of your labours which you have sown in the field; and the Feast of Ingathering at the end of the year, when you have gathered in* the fruit of *your labours from the field.*
> *17 Three times in the year all your males shall appear before the Lord GOD.*

Three times a year Jerusalem was filled with those who came from throughout the Jewish Diaspora to celebrate the three pilgrim feasts, Passover and Shavuot in the Spring and in the Autumn, Succoth.

Then with the outpouring of God's Holy Spirit on this same day of Shavuot, God spoke to the whole of Israel in their own languages through the one hundred and twenty disciples manifesting the gift of tongues. In this, God was preparing all Israel to receive His Messiah, Jesus of Nazareth, as Saviour and Lord.

There are also a surprisingly number of similarities between God giving of the Law to Moses and the giving of God's Holy Spirit on that Pentecost morn.

The law was given to Moses upon a high mountain.

God's Holy Spirit was given to the Disciples in the

upper room.

Thunder and lightning were heard by the Israelites below Mt Sinai.

There was the sound of a rushing wind and tongues of fire alighting on the disciples heads.

Voices were heard by the Israelites below Mt Sinai.

The worshipers who had come from countries from a far off to Jerusalem to celebrate Shavuot heard the Disciples speak in their own languages rejoicing at the coming of God's Holy Spirit.

Three thousand Israelites who rebelled and mocked Moses died that day (*Exodus 32:25-29*)

Three thousand Israelites readily responded to the Gospel message that day and were save and baptised (Acts 2:40-42)

God gave Moses a set of outward laws which would bind and hold the nation of Israel together.

God gave the one hundred and twenty disciples God's inward law of the Spirit that day, which would hold the Body of Christ together.

This Hebraic feast of Shavuot can therefore be seen to prophetically point forward to and link the Law of Moses to the coming of God's Holy at Pentecost.

Today, the spiritual significance of this Jewish festival reaches to the very core of both the Jewish and gentile Christian communities alike. And as a consequence of this, a full comprehension of the prophetic link between the Jewish faith and a belief and acceptance of Jesus as Messiah is inevitable.

FROM THE DAY OF PENTECOST ONWARDS

From the day of Pentecost, the numbers of believers in Jesus substantially increased. And with this development the Jewish Scribes and the Pharisees were greatly disturbed by what they saw and heard.

The early disciples soon became known as 'Followers of the Way' which reflected the words of Jesus, "I am the way, the truth and the life, no man comes to the Father except through Me." In this, the disciples were being drawn together into one new body, forming themselves into units of worship in their own right, similar in structure to that of the synagogue.

These Jewish believers began to touch the very fabric of their society, which the Jewish authorities considered totally unacceptable; and as a consequence, the authorities reacted to their behaviour and persecution followed.

THE CONVERSION OF PAUL

The tension between the Jewish authorities and the Jewish believers was further aggravated when Jewish believers began to bring uncircumcised gentiles into their midst, and at the same time did not separate themselves from the wider Jewish community. In response, the Jewish authorities attempted to further constrain the followers of Jesus in every way they saw fit.

Tragically, under the direct and specific direction of Saul of Tarsus, Stephen was martyred for his faith, the first disciple to die for the sake of the Gospel.

Acts 7:55-60
55 But he, being full of the Holy Spirit, gazed into heaven and saw the glory of God, and Jesus standing at the right hand of God,
56 and said, "Look! I see the heavens opened and the Son of Man standing at the right hand of God!"
57 Then they cried out with a loud voice, stopped their ears, and ran at him with one accord;
58 and they cast him out of the city and stoned him. And the witnesses laid down their clothes at the feet of a young man named Saul.
59 And they stoned Stephen as he was calling on God and saying, "Lord Jesus, receive my spirit."
60 Then he knelt down and cried out with a loud voice, "Lord, do not charge them with this sin." And when he had said this, he fell asleep.

Acts 8:1-4
1 Now Saul was consenting to his death. At that time a great persecution arose against the church which was at Jerusalem; and they were all scattered throughout the regions of Judea and Samaria, except the apostles.
2 And devout men carried Stephen to his burial, and made great lamentation over him.
3 As for Saul, he made havoc of the church, entering every house, and dragging off men and women, committing them to prison.
4 Therefore those who were scattered went everywhere preaching the word.

Following the stoning of Stephen, the followers of

Jesus fled into the surrounding countryside and as they scattered they passed the message of the Gospel on to the wider Jewish community and even on to the gentile Greek population at Antioch.

This was a time of great change in Antioch, especially as many Greek gentiles were converting to Judaism before they had ever heard about Jesus.

Then with Saul's dramatic conversion (Acts 9:1-31) a great commotion was stirred up amongst the followers of Jesus in Jerusalem. An extensive debate then arose as to how to accommodate this once persecutor of the faith. But Saul, now called Paul, had been chosen by God for a very specific ministry; this ministry was to reach out to the gentile communities throughout the known world.

Paul considered this calling to the gentiles as an awesome responsibility and he dedicated his life to the conversion and teaching of the gentile world. Yet during Paul's life he never neglected to preach the Gospel first to the Jewish community whenever the opportunity arose.

THE PROSELYTE

There were many gentiles who previously had converted to Judaism and then, through Paul's teaching, recognised and acknowledged Jesus as Messiah. The original conversion of these gentile proselyte to Judaism was no mean commitment and their acknowledgement of Jesus was to place them in a very unique position.

Within the community of believers, the converted Proselyte was able to form a bridge between the Jewish believer and the gentile believing community to such an extent that many gentiles, who having no previous contact with the Jewish community, also began to recognise and acknowledge the uniqueness of Jesus.

Those who recognised and accepted Jesus without first becoming Jewish proselytes knew little of Jewish ways and customs, and their lack of understanding of the Jewish faith resulted in many heated discussions between Jewish and gentile believers alike.

Sadly many of the Jewish/gentile conflicts that later arose were not resolved and even with Paul sending out letters of concern to the different believing communities, arguments and discussions have continued even to this day.

THE MYSTERY OF GOD - GOD IN US

This was the day the prophets of old looked forward to, to the day when God would intervene directly in Israel's history and in the affairs of Man, but how this intervention was to take place was a mystery to them.

The question arose: 'How could a holy God live in the company of fallen man?'

> *Matt 13:17*
> *17 "For assuredly I say unto you that many prophets and righteous men have desired to see what you see,*

and did not see it, and to hear what you hear, and did not hear."

It was God's desire to have an intimate and personal relationship with all who believed in Him, and with the coming of Jesus and the outpouring of God's Holy Spirit, God was able to enter and dwell within the centre of every true believer's being. This was the mystery of God, 'God in us the hope of glory'.

Mystery: From the Greek word (Musterion), meaning that which is known to the initiates; being outside the range of unassisted natural apprehension. (the understanding of a divine mystery through Divine revelation.) Scripture states - for a divine truth is made known through revelation.

With the coming of Messiah Jesus and the outpouring of God's Holy Spirit, the opportunity of a new way of living had come upon Israel.

Today, all people no matter their religious or cultural background have the same opportunity to respond to God and acknowledge Jesus as Messiah. All who accept Jesus enter into an intimate and personal relationship with God, and this relationship is but a foretaste of what is to come in all fullness at the end of the age.

1 Cor 2:9-10
9 But as it is written: "Eye has not seen, nor ear heard, Nor have entered into the heart of man The things which God has prepared for those who love Him."
10 But God has revealed them to us through His Spirit. For the Spirit searches all things, yes, the deep things of God.

All who accept Jesus enter into a kingdom that was established from before the foundation of the world and all who come to Him will be able to eat and drink of God's goodness and grace for all eternity.

THE EKKLESIA OF GOD

As time passed, the community of believers structured themselves into assemblies similar to the that of the synagogue, these assemblies became known in the Bible by their Greek name, Ekklesia.

EKKLESIA: From the Greek meaning - Assembly, from Ek, out of, and Klesis, a calling, i.e., the term Ekklesia meaning, 'The called out ones'.

As far as the Ekklesia is concerned, this was to be the format by which believers would come together to worship God.

With most translations of the Bible there is a tendency to replace this Greek word, Ekklesia, with the old English word, Church.

CHURCH: Old English, From the Greek word, Kuriakon (Doma) - the Lord's house, from

Kuriakos, of the master and Kurios meaning power.

And down through the ages the misunderstanding and misuse of power has been a major problem within the Christian church.

Unlike the formal structure of the synagogue, which required a minimum of ten men, a gathering of believers could be established on the basis of two or three people coming together in Jesus name.

THE FIRST MENTION OF THE EKKLESIA IN THE BIBLE

The first mention of the Ekklesia in the Bible was made by Jesus in the Gospel of Matthew:

> *Mat 16:13-20*
> *13 When Jesus came into the region of Caesarea Philippi, He asked His disciples, saying, "Who do men say that I, the Son of Man, am?"*
> *14 So they said, "Some say John the Baptist, some Elijah, and others Jeremiah or one of the prophets."*
> *15 He said to them, "But who do you say that I am?"*
> *16 Simon Peter answered and said, "You are the Christ, the Son of the living God."*
> *17 Jesus answered and said to him, "Blessed are you, Simon Bar-Jonah, for flesh and blood has not revealed this to you, but My Father who is in heaven.*
> *18 And I also say to you that you are Peter, and on this rock I will build My church, and the gates of Hades shall not prevail against it.*
> *19 And I will give you the keys of the kingdom of heaven, and whatever you bind on earth will be bound in heaven, and whatever you loose on earth will be loosed in heaven."*
> *20 Then He commanded His disciples that they should tell no one that He was Jesus the Christ.*

According to the above passage, there was to be an unceasing battle between the Ekklesia of God and the gates of Hades (or Hell). That is, the body of true believers who are dedicated and committed to their God and Saviour and who walk according to God's Spirit.

Therefore, since the time of Jesus this true Ekklesia has stood as a witness against the enemy for the purpose of restraining evil and its intent to destroy this world in which we live. This resistance of evil is worthy of note, especially where the identity of the Restrainer is concerned, as described in Paul's second letter to the believers at Thessalonica.

THE CHURCH, HELLENISM AND ISRAEL

At the time of Jesus, the Roman Empire dominated much of Europe and the Middle East, yet Greek/Hellenist culture continued to play a significant role in the life and thinking of Rome.

> *HELLENISM: The term Hellenism is derived from the name of an early Thessalonian King called Hellen and refers to the historic period 323 to 30 BC. Hellenism, along with its pagan and occult practices and traditions, was to prove one of the greatest stumbling blocks to the healthy growth of the early Church.*

The influence of this Greek/Hellenist philosophy brought gentile pagan thinking, belief and practice into the heart of the community of believers, and these beliefs and practices detrimentally affected the way the believers understood their relationship with God and the world in which they live.

The adoption of this Greek way of thinking also spiritualised the interpretation of Biblical Prophecy and consequently denied the literal interpretation of the prophetic word; this development turned the prophetic word it into no more than an allegorical tale.

To complicate issues yet further; at the time of Jesus there were many Jews within the Jewish community whose lifestyle had more in common with the gentile Greek/Hellenist world than with Judaism. Then when some of these Jewish Hellenists turned to Jesus, they too brought their influence to bear on the prophetic message and how it should be interpreted.

Over the following two and a half centuries a demographic change within the body of Christ took place. This change saw a decline in the number of Jewish believers in relation to the ever growing number of gentile believers. Then, without the Hebraic influence, the Church rapidly departed from the foundations of faith and this too had a dramatic effect on the understanding of the biblical prophetic word.

By the Third Century AD, the body of Christ had changed beyond all recognition. Following the reputed conversion of the Roman emperor, Constantine, and with Christianity being established as the state religion, the Church was forced to conform to Constantine's political ambitions and the true meaning of Ekklesia was again all but lost. This was certainly not what Jesus intended for His body of believers.

In the years ahead, the Church followed the same East West divide as the Roman Empire. In the West, the dominant church was the Church of Rome (the Roman Catholic Church) and in the East, the Orthodox Church. And over the following centuries both Churches followed and continued to be dominated by pagan Greek/Hellenist philosophy.

THE REFORMATION AND BEYOND

With the dawning of the sixteenth century a great change was about to take place within western Christendom. In Europe a religious revolution crossed the continent and this became known as the Reformation.

This Reformation was initiated in 1517 when Martin Luther, an Augustinian monk at the university of Wittenberg, declared that salvation was by faith alone and salvation could not be purchased by the buying of 'indulgences', that is, the buying of salvation, which the Church had been doing to raise funds. Luther also rallied the many within the Roman Catholic Church to demand change and the end to corruption.

During this Reformation period the spiritualised and allegorical approach to the understanding of the Bible was being seriously questioned; yet the prophetic word continued to be interpreted with a strong allegorical influence. But over the following centuries this too was going to change.

THE GREAT AWAKENING

In the early eighteenth century a Great Awakening swept through Europe and the Americas leaving a permanent impact on the church and all peoples it touched. This move of God concerned itself more with the state of a person's soul and required a personal response to this message from God. Through this awakening, awareness was raised for the need for serious social reform. This move of God was also ultimately responsible for the demise of the African slave trade.

THE NINETEENTH CENTURY ONWARD

By the time of the turbulent industrialisation of the 19th Century great change was once again taking place within the Christian church. During this time many Jews as well as gentiles saw the need for a Jewish homeland to be established somewhere in the world. But the consensus stated that this homeland could only be the land God gave to Abraham and his descendents.

During this time Great Britain and the USA saw a rapid growth of Christian outreach into the Jewish community, and this eventually becoming known as the Hebrew Christian Movement.

The 19th century also saw changes within the gentile

Christian community where the return to the foundations of faith were being ever more desired. Furthermore, during this time there was an intense focus on the prophetic message of the Bible, which brought two major avenues of concern to the fore:

First, the desire to see the nation of Israel returned to her ancient homeland.

Second, A growing interest in the study of the end times and the return of Jesus to earth.

Both aspects very much interrelated.

As part of this aspiration for a homeland for this disenfranchised nation of Israel, many leading figures, politicians and Bible scholars, such as J. N. Darby, Sir Robert Anderson and many others, also affirmed this need for a homeland for Israel recognising this to be central to the fulfilment of Biblical Prophecy.

ZIONISM – AND THE FIRST ZIONIST CONFERENCE

Within the Jewish community the longing for a homeland culminated in 1897 with the First Zionist Congress in Basel Switzerland.

This desire to establish an independent Israel in the Middle East, along with the need to promote national growth and development, became known and recognised worldwide as Zionism.

The term Zionism was first voiced in 1890 by Nathan Birnbaum (1864-1937) and emerged in response to the violent persecution of Jews in Eastern Europe and anti-

Semitism in the West.

ZIONISM: the yearning, desire and outworking of the Jewish nation to return to her ancestral and spiritual homeland. This desire has been embedded in Jewish culture, religious life, ritual and literature and prayer since the Jewish exile from the Land two thousand years ago

The ideology of Zionism therefore fuses the ancient Jewish biblical and historical ties to the ancestral Jewish homeland along with the desire for establishing a modem Jewish state in the land of Israel.

THE BASEL PROGRAM:-

With Theodor Herzl as president and Nathan Birnbaum elected Secretary General, the First Zionist Congress (1897) in Basel Switzerland laid out Zionism's goals which became known as the Basel Program.

The Basil Program was established to promote, by appropriate means, the settlement in the land of Israel, Jewish farmers, artisans, and manufacturers.

To organise and unite the whole of Jewry by means of appropriate institutions, both local and international in accordance with the laws of each country.

To strengthen and foster Jewish national sentiment and national consciousness.

To prepare steps toward obtaining the consent of governments, where necessary, in order to reach the goals of Zionism.

Theodor Herzl

Austrian journalist Theodor Herzl has been considered as the "father" of modern Zionism. Herzl consolidated various strands of Zionist thought into an organised political movement. Herzl saw this Jewish question as an international political question to be dealt with in the arena of international politics.

Herzl advocated international recognition of a Jewish homeland, the location of which was not important to Herzl, but subsequent pressure would strongly indicate that there was only one homeland for the Jewish nation and that was the land of Israel.

Then Fifty years later, in May 1948, the establishment of the State of Israel fulfilled this Jewish desire for the restoration of Israel.

NATHAN BIRNBAUM

Lesser known, Nathan Birnbaum, played a prominent role in the First Zionist Congress (1897) and was elected Secretary General of the Zionist Organisation. However, Birnbaum and Herzl developed ideological differences with Birnbaum beginning to question the political aims of Zionism.

Birnbaum began to attach increasing importance to the national-cultural intent of Judaism which eventually caused him to embrace full traditional Judaism. His work and effort eventually led toward a Jewish spiritual revival.

This conflict of thought between Theodor Herzl and Nathan Birnbaum caused them to part company, this being very common within great idealistic ventures. Yet the vision of both these great men was necessary for the establishment of Israel in her ancient homeland, and this gave Israel back her spiritual heart and soul, dry bones arising from death.

Following the first Zionist Congress in 1897, Theodore Herzl stated he believed the establishment of the State of Israel, in the Middle East, would take place within 50 years. Exactly 50 years later in 1948, with the authority of the United Nations, the State of Israel was born and recognised by the majority of nations around the globe.

The creation of this State of Israel has been possibly one of the greatest prophetic and political miracles in world history, all foretold over 2000 years ago in the Hebrew scripture.

THE FIRST AND SECOND WORLD WARS

Following on the heels of the First Zionist Congress, the twentieth century saw both the First and Second World Wars having a specific impact on the creation of the State of Israel.

Then as a direct consequence of World War One, the British Government stated there was an essential requirement for a homeland for the Jewish people.

As a direct consequence of the Second World War, the creation of that homeland for Israel came to pass.

Once again Israel has been reborn and rebuilt in troubled times.

THE FIRST WORLD WAR

The First World War caught Great Britain totally unprepared. At the onset of World War I, Britain found herself running out of acetone which was used in the production of the explosive Cordite for the manufacture of munitions. At this time, Winston Churchill, First Lord of the Admiralty approached Dr Chaim Weizmann, an exceptionally gifted Jewish chemist, for help. Dr Weizmann went on to develop a method for synthesising acetone which was then used in the production of Cordite, this resulted in the success of the war effort.

In response for this help the British Government asked Dr Weizmann how they could ever repay him. Dr Weisman requested the British Government assist with the re-establishment of a Jewish homeland in the Middle East; then towards the end of World War 1, with the pronouncement of the Balfour Declaration, this promise to Israel was fulfilled.

THE SECOND WORLD WAR

The Second World War brought an intensely serious and sinister impact upon the Jewish people of Europe. This war, created by Hitler, was constructed and engineered with the deliberate foresight, intention and framework to completely wipe out the Jewish nation.

With over six million Jewish men, women and children slaughtered in this Holocaust, the extent, intensity and thoroughness of this specifically planned genocide had never been seen or attempted by any country before.

We often think of 6,000,000 Jews being systematically murdered but do not really comprehend the extent of this carnage. On average over a six year period 1,000,000 Jews per year were slaughtered, or 83,000 Jews per month every month for 6 years. On a weekly basis that is just over 19,000 Jews per week died, 2,700 each day.

We saw national and international shock resulting from the Columbine High School shooting. Now consider one complete US high school massacre happening each and every day for six years across the USA, but this time each school being totally decimated.

To attempt to reflect on the magnitude and the effect of this slaughter on a daily basis is beyond comprehension. How a nation such as Israel could cope with this onslaught is incomprehensible, yet Israel survived

CHAPTER 5.

....

ONE NEW NATION – ONE NEW MAN

ONE NATION

With the founding of the State of Israel in 1948, many Christians believe the biblical prophetic message can be interpreted from a more literal perspective. And this is believed to reflect the heart of God and His love for His people which is founded upon God's eternal covenant with Abraham.

God's heart can be heard in the following verses.

> *Matt 23:37-39*
> *37 Jerusalem, Jerusalem, the one who kills the prophets and stones those who are sent to her! How often I wanted to gather your children together, as a hen gathers her chicks under her wings, but you were not willing!*
> *38 See! Your house is left to you desolate;*
> *39 for I say to you, you shall see Me no more till you say, 'Blessed is He who comes in the name of the Lord!'*

ABRAHAM AND THE FOUNDING OF ISRAEL

While settled in Ur in the land of the Chaldees, God called Abraham to go with his family to the land of Canaan. In this, God made a commitment to Abraham, known as the Abrahamic Covenant (Genesis Ch 11-13).

This commitment was an eternal covenant between God and Abraham and his seed forever. God promised Abraham that his family would flourish and his descendents would become a great nation and they would number as the stars in the night sky.

From that time and for almost two thousand years God guided and directed the descendents of Abraham and appointed them Judges and Prophets to nurture and guide His people until the coming of Messiah.

The vast majority of the judges and prophets were faithful in their calling and expected every word God gave them to come to pass. One of these great prophets was Ezekiel, and he had much to say to Israel and more specifically to the house of Judah.

FROM SOLOMON TO THE BABYLONIAN EXILE

Following the death of king Solomon, Israel split into two factions, ten tribes to the north, collectively known as Israel or to be more precise, Ephraim. In the south, the remaining two tribes were collectively as Judah.

The House of Israel consisted of the tribes of Reuben

Simeon Dan Naphtali Gad Asher Issachar Zebulun Manasseh Ephraim

The House of Judah consisted of the tribes of Benjamin Judah.

Please note: For this listing of the tribes of Israel, the tribe of Levi, the priestly clan, has not been included in the dividing of the land, but the tribe of Levi was allocated cities and land throughout Israel and Judah where they could live and have for their own use.

REBELLION

The ten northern tribes continued to rebel against God and as a consequence, they were taken captive into exile in Assyria. Later, the two southern tribes, Judah and Benjamin, were also taken into captivity, but this time to Babylon. In this the whole house of Israel and Judah fell.

During the harrowing time of Judah's exile, God clearly spoke to the Prophet Ezekiel.

Ezekiel was the son of Buzi (Ezek 1:3), a Prophet of God and was born into the priestly Kohan family.

In the year 597 BC Ezekiel along with king Jehoiachin, king of Judah and many men and woman and children were taken captive to Babylon by king Nebuchadnezzar. And there in Babylon Ezekiel received his visions.

Towards the end of the Book of Ezekiel (Chapter 36), God states that Israel and Judah would one day return to their own land, all be it in unbelief, and in modern times this return has continued since the early part of the last century.

God then revealed to Ezekiel that the re-awakening and restoration of the House of Israel and the House of Judah and their coming together as one body united, would truly take place. This was an event not considered possible until Israel, as a nation, was re-gathered and re-established back in her ancestral homeland.

According to Ezekiel (Chapter 37), God then gives Ezekiel a vision, a valley with dry bones rising up and coming together, along with sinew and flesh and life being breathed upon them. In this, we are presented with a dilemma; except for the partial return home of the tribes of Judah and Benjamin from the Babylonian exile, there has been no time in Israel's history in which this prophecy been fulfilled.

In this chapter, God then caused Ezekiel to walk around the bones and asked him, "Son of man, can these bones live?" and Ezekiel answered, "O Lord God, You know."

God then proceeds to instruct Ezekiel to prophecy to the dry bones commanding them to hear the word of the Lord. "Surely I will cause breath to enter into you, and you shall live. I will put sinews on you and bring flesh upon you, cover you with skin and put breath in you; and you shall live. Then you shall know that I am the Lord." (Ezek. 37:3-4)

When Ezekiel prophesied and commanded the bones to live, they began rattling and coming together. Sinews and flesh were wrapped upon the bones and skin was then wrapped upon the sinews and flesh. God now commands Ezekiel to prophecy life into the bones that they may live. In doing so, the bones arose and stood up on their feet as an exceedingly great army.

God then specifically tells Ezekiel these bones represent the whole House of Israel, Ephraim and Judah united, and that they are dry and that they are aware their hope is lost and they themselves are cut off from God.

Ezekiel was once again called to prophesy and this time say to the bones:

> *Ezek 37:12-14*
> *12....'Thus says the Lord God: "Behold, O My people, I will open your graves and cause you to come up from your graves, and bring you into the land of Israel.*
> *13 Then you shall know that I am the Lord, when I have opened your graves, O My people, and brought you up from your graves.*
> *14 I will put My Spirit in you, and you shall live, and I will place you in your own land. Then you shall know that I, the Lord, have spoken it and performed it,"*
> *says the Lord.'"*

What a hope, what a promise, God stated He would completely restore the whole House of Israel, Ephraim and Judah together, and place them back in their own land, and this would be done in a time such as this. During this time, the whole house of Israel would once again come to know her God and know it was He who brought her back home to the land God promised them.

It has always been God's intention to bring the house of Israel (Ephraim) and Judah together as one nation, that they would no longer defile themselves with idols and there would be no more transgression:

"*for they shall be My people, and I will be their God.*"

In this we see the Messianic promise of a coming king and God would make an eternal covenant of peace with Israel and Judah, they would prosper and God would dwell in their midst forever.

ISRAEL'S RESPONSE TODAY

Today vast numbers from around the world are returning to their ancient homeland. Many of folk are also returning from Middle Eastern countries including Yemeni Jews who are descendents of Israelites who settled in the Saudi Arabian peninsula from before the time of Solomon. Others returnees include Moroccan and Ethiopian Jews along with Jews from many other Arabic countries and beyond.

With this repatriation, Israel can be seen being brought together as one nation, and this in complete fulfilment of Scripture. The modem state of Israel can be truly seen as a living example of biblical prophecy coming to pass in a literal and true fashion.

ISRAEL'S RE-GATHERING AND RECOGNITION OF MESSIAH

Through Israel returning to her ancient homeland the scene is now set for the next great fulfilling of God's prophetic word.

> *Ezek 37:25*
> *25 Then they shall dwell in the land that I have given to Jacob My servant, where your fathers dwelt; and they shall dwell there, they, their children, and their children's children, forever; and My servant David shall be their prince forever.*

And with God's promise to Israel and Judah, a time will soon to come when all Israel will recognise, acknowledge and accept Yeshua as Messiah. This being a promise which would appear almost impossible in a day and age such as this. But it is often in difficult and strange times that God acts unexpectedly.

JEWISH AND GENTILE BELIEVERS TODAY – ONE BODY

As part of this restoration of Israel and a growing community of Jewish believers around the world, Jewish and gentile believers alike are presented with major issues which require addressing:

Has the foundation of the modern State of Israel been an accident of history or has it been part of God's unfolding of plan for His people and the world at large?

And should the believing community, Jew and

gentile alike, assist in fulfilling biblical prophecy, or should this be left specifically and solely to God?

From the above, two further questions arise, this time involving the 'Right of Return':

Should the believing community, be practically, spiritually or even politically involved in assisting the Jewish/Israelite community to return to Israel?

And is there a valid biblical and prophetic, historical and political reason to support and assist the modern State of Israel?

A BODY DIVIDED

Those who believe in the continued existence of the modern State of Israel in the Middle East are divided into many different factions within both Jewish and gentile communities, with all being motivated by differing ideologies.

For many Jews (both Orthodox and non-Orthodox) and gentiles (Christian and non-Christian alike), biblical prophecy and the modem State of Israel are in no way related, that is, the existence of the physical State of Israel and the spiritual declaration of God's word are entirely separate issues. Yet nearly all Jewish believers and a proportion of the gentile believing community consider the uniting of Bible prophecy and the establishment of the modem State of Israel to be at the heart of God's and plan for the Middle East today.

Surprisingly, many within the Orthodox and ultra-

Orthodox Jewish communities consider the existence of the political state of Israel as an anathema and state that the re-establishment of the nation of Israel should not be recognised until after the coming of Messiah.

Also within the Orthodox community, it is argued that with the State of Israel welcoming secular and non-Orthodox Jews and gentiles into the land, the promise God made to Israel has been considerably weakened.

For those gentiles who oppose the existence of the State of Israel are generally anti-Zionist by nature and often use anti-Zionism as a euphemism to promote anti-Semitic rhetoric and speech.

Sadly, for both Jewish and gentile believers who recognise Jesus as Messiah and who long for His return, there continues to be vehement debate and difference of opinion with respect to many aspects of Jewish/Christian relations.

At a time such as this, when true believers in Messiah Jesus should be standing together in unison, there is unnecessary division and for the sake of the Gospel this situation must be resolved.

ONE FURTHER ISSUE

'How do gentile believers relate to an Israel who does not walk fully in the light of her God?"

One solution can be found from looking at scripture. The Bible tells us that gentile nations will help Israel return to her land while she is yet in unbelief (Ezekiel) and support Israel in her struggle for peace and security (Isaiah).

Therefore the establishment of the modern State of Israel, by the will of God and by His desire and by His hand can be clearly seen to come to pass. And through a 'three stranded cord', God's word is coming true:

i Without God's prophetic declaration, the modern State of Israel would never have come into being.

ii. Without the continued struggle by Israel and her own self belief and limited faith in God, Israel would not have come to life.

iii. Without the political will from Israel's gentile allies, Israel would remain totally isolated and become choked by the surrounding nations.

Therefore, it is my strongest conviction that the modern State of Israel and the political developments relating to Israel and the Middle East are coming to pass as a direct and specific result of God's faithfulness and promise to Israel. And in turn, is the fulfilment of Bible Prophecy.

A LOOK TO THE FUTURE

In Israel today the wakeup call is sounding, but sadly a very large percentage of Israelis have no time for spiritual matters. Therefore, on a political front, the only way forward for Israel would be to adopt a secular solution for the solving of its problems. Those who choose this secular route will be sorely disappointed.

Each and every time the nation of Israel has taken a secular route all has not bode well for the country. And with this secular route the road map for peace will literally become a road map to hell.

As a consequence of this secular route, Israel will eventually shake hands with the most deceitful and evil political leader this world 'has ever known. The Book of Revelation describes this leader as 'the Beast', otherwise known as 'Antichrist' or as Daniel calls him, 'the Man of Sin', and this man's ambition will be to wipe Israel off the face of the earth.

In contrast, compared to this coming 'Man of Sin' Hitler will appear to have been a congenial friend to Israel.

According to Daniel this future enemy of God will surreptitiously set out to destroy Israel, as did Hitler. Initially this Man of Sin will appear to be a friend to Israel and at an opportune moment he will then turn viciously upon the nation, making one final concerted effort to destroy the nation. When Israel realizes her mistake, it will be too late, the enemy will have invaded the Land and made a very serious attempt to take complete control of Israel.

The Bible does not state why Israel will accept this Man of Sin, but there is a suggestion in the Gospels that Israel will once again will have to choose between accepting the true Saviour and a false saviour. This is very reminiscent when the crowds chose Barabbas over Jesus. Sadly, at the time of the end the wrong choice will be made, and only through one further period of suffering will Israel eventually accept the One who comes in the name of the Lord.

Thankfully Daniel records that this Man of Sin will not have complete dominion over the Middle East. For God has prepared a 'Cleft in the Rock' for all who will hear and who obey His voice, and those folk who listen to God will have the opportunity to escape the coming great and terrible day.

In that 'Cleft in the Rock' Israel will meet and commune with her God and acknowledge Yeshua not only as Messiah, but also as Lord and Master and coming King.

ONE NEW MAN

Today, there is great resistance within the Jewish community to accept Jesus as Messiah and this partly rises out of a misunderstanding of the nature of faith. According to the Jewish community, when a Jewish person accepts Jesus as Messiah, he or she is believed to have abandoned his or her faith and people. I would strongly suggest this is not the case.

When a member of the Jewish community accepts Jesus as Messiah, the Jewish believer remains thoroughly Jewish and there is no biblical basis for this not to be the case. For the Jewish believer, what has been ritual becomes a remembrance celebration and the full meaning of every aspect of Jewish life takes on new depth and understanding.

WHO ARE GOD'S PEOPLE

In recent years many Jewish and gentile believers alike have continued to find the integration of their communities very difficult, and this has caused questions to arise, especially out of division of culture.

At the time of Paul, the most prominent question being asked, "Is it possible for a gentile to be admitted into the community of God without first being admitted into the community of Israel? This issue proved to be a serious threat to the freedom of the Gospel and was finally resolved at the Jerusalem Council as described in Acts, Ch. 15.

Today the question is precisely the opposite; the question now being asked is, "Can a Jewish person become a follower of Jesus without first becoming a gentile? The answer to this question is much the same as the same as the answer to the previous.

REPLACEMENT THEOLOGY

Replacement Theology has had a serious detrimental effect on the body of believers. This teaching believes God has completely rejected Israel in favour of the Church. Therefore, the Church has replaced Israel in God's plans and purposes for this world.

As a consequence of this belief, all Bible prophecy is

now considered to relate to the church, with Israel having no place in the economy of God. Regrettably Replacement Theology is rampant within many Christian organizations and denominations, especially through Dominionism, Reconstructionism, Kingdom Now and the Restoration movement.

THE OLIVE TREE

As the Hebraic foundations of the Christian faith continue to be examined, the question also arises, "Who therefore are God's people?"

For many gentile Christians, this question is totally irrelevant, but to those working within the Jewish community or who are coming into contact with Jewish believers, this question is of vital importance.

The olive tree analogy of Romans Chapter 11 casts crucial light on the above question.

> *Rom 11:24-26*
> *24 For if you were cut out of the olive tree which is wild by nature, and were grafted contrary to nature into a cultivated olive tree, how much more will these, who are natural branches, be grafted into their own olive tree?*
> *25 For I do not desire, brethren, that you should be ignorant of this mystery, lest you should be wise in your own opinion, that blindness in part has happened to Israel until the fullness of the Gentiles has come in. 26 And so all Israel will be saved, as it is written: "The Deliverer will come out of Zion, And He will turn away ungodliness*

from Jacob;

The most common theology within Judaism would answer this question, the Jewish people are God's people. And the most common theology in Christendom would state the members of the Church are God's people.

The Olive Tree analogy is possibly the only solution that can bridge the gap between Jewish and gentile believers, thus fulfilling the promise of Jesus, "That they may be one."

As far as the olive tree is considered, there are two distinct groups of people, both who in some respect are part of God's community, and no proper and complete theology can ignore either of them:

The Jewish community being the cultivated olive tree. Many of branches of this cultivated olive tree have fallen off; the branches that have fallen off can be grafted back on.

The gentile Christian community being the wild olive branches that have been grafted into the cultivated olive tree. According to Paul, these wild branches can just as easily fall or be broken off.

This Olive Tree approach to the understanding of God's relationship with his people greatly helps to counteract the growing anti-Semitism and influence of Replacement Theology within the majority of the gentile Church.

With Christians understanding and adopting this Olive Tree approach, they can root out all remnants of anti-Semitism from the Church, and this will assist in countering the rising tide of anti-Semitism within the wider society.

COMING TOGETHER OF JEWISH AND GENTILE BELIEVERS

Today, God is at work within both the Jewish and gentile believing community uniting them into one family known as the Bride of Jesus. Through the joining of Jewish and gentile believers, the true bride can be seen arising out of the debris of all that purports to follow Him.

Furthermore, the relationship between Jewish and gentile believers was central to the teachings of Paul and very much reflects the words of Jesus in His prayer in the Gospel of John (Ch. 17), "that they may be one as we are one".

Today God is truly speaking to all Israel, but if the predominantly gentile Church does not listen, recognise and positively respond to this call and make provision for it, then some of those wild olive branches so carefully grafted in will once again be broken off. In this I am not referring to an individual believer's salvation, but referring to the predominantly gentile church requiring to recognize God's call to Israel and God's ongoing plan of salvation for the Israelite nation.

CHAPTER 6.

....

UNDERSTANDING THE PROPHETIC TEXT

This section outlines some basic principles for the interpretation of biblical prophecy, and hopefully this will assist the reader in undertaking a consistent interpretation of the prophetic text.

First and foremost, for those who accept the Bible as the complete Word of God, the following statements are declared as being true.

1. The whole Bible, both Old and New Testament together, is totally complete within itself.

2. The biblical prophetic message is totally consistent and reliable.

3. The Bible contains all things necessary for life and salvation.

With the Word of God being known to be true,

Scripture can be studied with confidence.

FIGURATIVE LANGUAGE AND THE SELF INTERPRETATION OF SCRIPTURE

When the Pioneer space probes were sent out to the outer extremities of our solar system, plaques were placed on the side of the probes. These plaques gave details of the location and intent of the human race. The plaques were designed in such way as to allow any supposed alien space traveller to decipher them.

As I considered these plaques, I wondered if the Bible also contained inbuilt instructions, or had its own keys for unlocking the prophetic scriptures contained in the Bible.

Rev 1:12-18
12 Then I turned to see the voice that spoke with me. And having turned I saw seven golden lampstands,
13 and in the midst of the seven lampstands One like the Son of Man, clothed with a garment down to the feet and girded about the chest with a golden band.
14 His head and hair were white like wool, as white as snow, and His eyes like a flame of fire;
15 His feet were like fine brass, as if refined in a furnace, and His voice as the sound of many waters;
16 He had in His right hand seven stars, out of His mouth went a sharp two-edged sword, and His countenance was like the sun shining in its strength.
17 And when I saw Him, I fell at His feet as dead. But He laid His right hand on me, saying to me, "Do not be afraid; I am the First and the Last.
18 I am He who lives, and was dead, and behold, I am alive forevermore. Amen. And I have the keys of Hades and of Death.
Rev 1:19-20

19 Write the things which you have seen, and the things which are, and the things which will take place after this.
20 The mystery of the seven stars which you saw in My right hand, and the seven golden lampstands: The seven stars are the angels of the seven churches, and the seven lampstands which you saw are the seven churches.

The first chapter of the Book of Revelation contains a clear example of this principle of self explanation and the use of figurative language to illustrate an actual event.

Verses 12-18 contain a description of Jesus walking in the midst of the seven golden lampstands, then verses 19-20 proceed to give the meaning of the vision. In this, a picture or figurative language is used to illustrate a specific and actual event, that is, Jesus walking among the seven churches in Asia Minor.

If John saw Jesus walk amongst the actual seven churches in Asia Minor, I wonder how long it would have taken John to describe what he saw? One other example of this figurative use of language is one image describing only one person, such as Jesus being described as the Lamb of God; no other person has this title.

If a consistent approach to the interpretation of biblical prophecy were adopted, many of the seeming conflicts within the prophetic text would not occur.

TEXT, CONTEXT AND PRETEXT

Another important aspect for the correct interpretation of biblical prophecy is that of the correct understanding of language, especially the use of the terms such as, Text, Context and Pretext. For example, a Bible text taken out of context becomes a pretext.

TEXT:

Definition: The main body of a printed or written work as distinct from commentary or notes.

CONTEXT:

Definition: Part of a piece of writing or speech that proceeds and or follows a word or phrase and contributes to its full meaning.

PRETEXT:

Definition: A text taken out of context or a fictitious reason given in order to conceal the real one, a spurious excuse.

TYPES AND SYMBOLS

Most problems associated with the interpretation of biblical prophecy can be eliminated if the student is consistent in the use of types and symbols and stays within the biblical context of the said type or symbol.

TYPE:-

Throughout scripture we read of types of Christ, that is, characters in the Bible who exhibit aspects of the character and nature of Christ or Messiah. These types are examples of the anti-type to come at a later date.

For example:-

Joshua has often been portrayed as a type of Christ or Messiah, i.e. a saviour of his people, Joshua being the type, with Christ or Messiah being the root or anti-type.

In this usage, the term anti-type is a grammatical term and differs in usage from terms such as, Antichrist, which means against or opposed to Christ.

For Jewish believers in Yeshua, the term anti-Messiah would be more appropriate, but due to such common usage of the term Antichrist I will use this term throughout this publication.

SYMBOL:-

From the first page of the Book of Genesis to the last page of the Book of Revelation, symbols are used in a representative manner.   And as we look to the prophetic message, figurative language is also used to record incidents and events which could not otherwise be described by the observer.

For example:-

Bread and Wine being representative of the body and blood of Jesus; the description of seven Lampstands or Menorah in the Book of Revelation, where each lampstand represents one of the seven churches in Asia Minor. Figurative language can also represent people and/or situations.

CHANGING USAGE OF LANGUAGE

With the continued development of language, some words and phrases change meaning, and in the case of prophetic scripture this needs to be addressed. Books such as Vine's Expository Dictionary of New Testament Words, the Amplified Bible and Stern's Jewish Bible are three of the many reference books that can prove to be very useful in assisting us to have a greater understanding of God's word.

THE PROPHETS AND PATTERNS IN BIBLICAL PROPHECY

When the Word of the Lord was given to the prophet it often had a direct application relevant to the people of the time; the Word would then point forward to a future date and then possibly onto an ultimate fulfilment at the end of the age.

And finally, with this short introduction for the interpretation of Bible prophecy, it is therefore possible to consider the prophetic and apocalyptic books of the Bible in a more literal, straightforward and consistent manner

CHAPTER 7.

....

TWO LETTERS TO THE BELIEVERS AT THESSALONICA

INTRODUCTION

Before considering the prophetic books of the bible, there is a need to consider the two letters Paul sent to the believers at Thessalonica. Paul wrote these two letters to comfort and encourage the saints living in this city during a time of great difficulty and persecution. Through these letters Paul also deals with many issues related to the time of the end.

Prior to Paul writing, some unknown person had greatly upset the believers by stating that the day of God's wrath had already come. In his letters Paul proceeds to make every effort to allay their fears and inform them that God will keep them from the day of His wrath.

These two letters also give a detailed insight into a series of events that will lead up to the day of the revealing of the Man of Sin, otherwise known as Antichrist. This revelation also provides us with the theological basis for the belief in the Resurrection and Ascension of the Saints, otherwise known as the Rapture.

Today, as in the days of this early church, false teachers continue to make every effort to creep in and deceiving many, causing some believers to fall away. During times like these, God commanded us not to be deceived and to continue to live productive and fruitful lives and to remain faithful to the end of our days. In this Jesus will say on that last day, "Well done, good and faithful servant."

The believers at Thessalonica were also deeply concerned about what happens to those who die before Jesus returns. Paul again assures the believers that those who have died in Christ are at peace and would arise to meet with Jesus at the end of the age, and so we are commanded not to worry.

In Chapter three, Paul again declares his ongoing concern for the suffering and persecution of the believers, he tells them he could no longer be apart from them and so he will send Timothy to be with them in their time of trial. Paul continues to pray for the saints night and day, praying that whatever was lacking in their faith would be strengthened and that God's blessing would be upon them.

We now have the first inkling of Paul's understanding of the return of Jesus, without which it would be difficult to assemble the jigsaw that reveals what will come to pass as the time of Jesus return draws near.

> *1 Thess 3:11-13*
> *11 Now may our God and Father Himself, and our Lord Jesus Christ, direct our way to you.*
> *12 And may the Lord make you increase and abound in love to one another and to all, just as we do to you,*
> *13 so that He may establish your hearts blameless in holiness before our God and Father at the coming of our Lord Jesus Christ with all His saints.*

During this coming time there is a need for the believer to stand blameless and holy before God. For God has called us not to wait to put right all that we can. The first step in this process is to allow our love to abound more and more towards God and towards each other; thus God will establish our hearts blameless and holy before Him and in this to make us ready for the return of His Son.

Chapter 4: Summary of verses 1-12

Paul now exhorts the believers to be filled more and more with God's grace and encourages them to walk in faith. Paul continues to encourage the believers to live pure and holy lives, to abstain from anything which would interfere with their relationship with God and warns them to live quiet lives minding their own business; not to be busybodies, to work faithfully with their own hands and not exploit any other person in the midst of their problems.

ay we have the opportunity to correct our ways and our thinking before it is too late. For God desires a true pure and contrite heart and this more so as the day of Jesus' return draws ever closer.

THE RAPTURE OF THE SAINTS OF GOD

There is also a need to consider possibly one of the most controversial aspect about the study of the End Times, the Rapture of the Saints of God.

> *1 Thess 4:13-17*
> *13 But I do not want you to be ignorant, brethren, concerning those who have fallen asleep, lest you sorrow as others who have no hope.*
> *14 For if we believe that Jesus died and rose again, even so God will bring with Him those who sleep in Jesus.*
> *15 For this we say to you by the word of the Lord, that we who are alive and remain until the coming of the Lord will by no means precede those who are asleep.*
> *16 For the Lord Himself will descend from heaven with a shout, with the voice of an archangel, and with the trumpet of God. And the dead in Christ will rise first. 17 Then we who are alive and remain shall be caught up together with them in the clouds to meet the Lord in the air. And thus we shall always be with the Lord.*

FROM GREEK TO LATIN

The term Rapture is not used in the bible, but this term is a perfectly valid way to describe the Resurrection and Ascension of the Saints at the end of the age.

Rapture: its meaning and significance.

Harpazo: The original Greek word - meaning: to seize, snatch or carry away (caught up).

Rapio: The original Latin word - also meaning: to seize, snatch or carry away.

Rapture: From the Old English meaning'. to transport a person from one place to another. Coming from the Latin word - Rapio.

From the above, the word 'Rapture' can be directly substituted into the above verse, with the 'Rapture of the believers' being a direct scriptural definition of our gathering together to be with Jesus.

The Rapture of the saints will take place, but the day and the hour will remain a mystery until we are caught up to be with Jesus. We can therefore be confident that at the end of the age all those who are truly born of the Spirit of God will be gathered together to be with Jesus for all eternity.

Many sound bible teachers hold to different opinions as to when this Rapture of the Saints will take place. Some believe it will happen before the time of Tribulation, some during and others at the end. And some do not believe it will happen at all.

Although I warm towards a pre-Tribulation rapture, one of my favourite evangelists and End Times bible teachers believes the rapture will take place at the mid-way point during the time of Tribulation. Added to this, one of my mentors who has helped review this manuscript over the years believes in a post-Tribulation rapture.

Sadly, the position taken on the timing of the Rapture has divided many Christians. This division is completely unnecessary and intensely destructive. Whenever the Rapture takes place, God has warned us to be ready at all times.

For those who believe in a pre-Tribulation rapture, all who have been born of the Spirit of God and who have turned from their sin will be taken to be with Jesus, not one true believer will be left behind. At this time, at the beginning of the seven years of Tribulation, many of those who have been left behind will realize their mistake, repent and turn to God. These folk will have a very important role to play during the following seven years.

An emerging consensus within the Jewish Messianic community would suggest a growing belief in a post-Tribulation rapture. The reason for this conviction arises out of two main beliefs.

The first results from a conviction that we are presently living in the time of Tribulation.

The second reason results from the desire not to leave family, friends or neighbours behind as would happen with a pre or a mid-Tribulation rapture.

In relation to the first conviction, we are certainly not

living in the time of Tribulation. The time of Tribulation specifically begins with the identification of Antichrist and the signing of the seven year treaty and this has not yet taken place.

In relation to the second conviction, not only Jewish family members and relations who are not born again will be left behind but this also apply to gentile believer, we are all literally in the same boat.

I would like to suggest that when the time of the Rapture comes, it may only be the shock of a pre-Tribulation rapture that will cause family and friends to turn and acknowledge Yeshua/Jesus as Messiah, if this is the case, then God will have a very specific job for these Tribulation saints before Jesus finally returns.

As far as escapism is concerned, "Who ever said the time leading up to the time of Tribulation was going to any easier than the time of Tribulation itself?"

One further issue which the believers at Thessalonica found difficult was their concern for those who had fallen asleep. In other words, for those people who had died. Paul encourages the believers to take hope because no believer who dies before Jesus returns or live to see Him return, will be disappointed.

> *1 Thess 4:13-17*
> *13 But I do not want you to be ignorant, brethren, concerning those who have fallen asleep, lest you sorrow as others who have no hope.*
> *14 For if we believe that Jesus died and rose again, even so God will bring with Him those who sleep in Jesus.*

*15 For this we say to you by the word of the Lord,
that we who are alive and remain until the coming of
the Lord will by no means precede those who are
asleep.
16 For the Lord Himself will descend from heaven
with a shout, with the voice of an archangel, and with
the trumpet of God. And the dead in Christ will rise
first.
17 Then we who are alive and remain shall be caught
up together with them in the clouds to meet the Lord
in the air. And thus we shall always be with the Lord.*

Thankfully, the words of the bible are true and the promise given to the early disciples is just as valid today as it was two thousand years ago.

CHAPTER 5

On reading through the prophetic aspects of Paul's writing, there is a distinct impression that Paul was expecting the imminent return of Jesus. Today the same expectation has arisen and the very same words are being declared today and declared with the same drive and passion that drove the early apostle.

*1 Thess 5:1-8
1   But concerning the times and the seasons,
brethren, you have no need that I should write to
you.
2 For you yourselves know perfectly that the day of
the Lord so comes as a thief in the night.
3   For when they say, "Peace and safety!" then
sudden destruction comes upon them, as labour pains
upon a pregnant woman. And they shall not escape.
4 But you, brethren, are not in darkness, so that this
Day should overtake you as a thief.*

5 You are all sons of light and sons of the day. We are not of the night nor of darkness.
6 Therefore let us not sleep, as others do, but let us watch and be sober.
7 For those who sleep, sleep at night, and those who get drunk are drunk at night.
8 But let us who are of the day be sober, putting on the breastplate of faith and love, and as a helmet the hope of salvation.

Paul now assures the brethren that they already know what will happen as the time of the end approaches and he encourages them to take confidence and trust God. Today we have two thousand years of history behind Paul's letters and every word has remained true and can be fully trusted.

The Coming Judgement

Today the world has the opportunity to change but this opportunity will not last forever, God's judgement on this world will come and catch the world unprepared. And Paul continues to warns us to be ready and prepared at all times for Jesus return, because Jesus has called us to discipleship and commitment and be radical in our approach to the way we live.

1 Thess 5:9-11
9 For God did not appoint us to wrath, but to obtain salvation through our Lord Jesus Christ,
10 who died for us, that whether we wake or sleep, we should live together with Him.
11 Therefore comfort each other and edify one another, just as you also are doing.

Through God's word, Paul continues to encourages the

saints by stating the judgement of God is not for the believer but for those who have turned away from God. This judgement will in particular fall upon those who have persecuted Israel, for God continues to love His chosen people and He will not betray them nor will He fail to keep His promise to the descendents of Abraham.

> *1 Thess 5:12-15*
> *12 And we urge you, brethren, to recognize those who labour among you, and are over you in the Lord and admonish you,*
> *13 and to esteem them very highly in love for their work's sake. Be at peace among yourselves.*
> *14 Now we exhort you, brethren, warn those who are unruly, comfort the fainthearted, uphold the weak, be patient with all.*
> *15 See that no one renders evil for evil to anyone, but always pursue what is good both for yourselves and for all.*

Even in the troubled times of the first century, Paul encouraged all who believe to work in complete unity, to support the weak and to be patient with one another, in this, Paul shows great concern for the welfare of the total person, spirit, soul and body and his desire is that all believers may be preserved blameless at the coming of our Lord Jesus Christ.

> *1 Thess 5:16-28*
> *16 Rejoice always,*
> *17 pray without ceasing,*
> *18 in everything give thanks; for this is the will of God in Christ Jesus for you.*
> *19 Do not quench the Spirit.*
> *20 Do not despise prophecies.*

21 Test all things; hold fast what is good.
22 Abstain from every form of evil.
23 Now may the God of peace Himself sanctify you completely; and may your whole spirit, soul, and body be preserved blameless at the coming of our Lord Jesus Christ.
24 He who calls you is faithful, who also will do it.
25 Brethren, pray for us.
26 Greet all the brethren with a holy kiss.
27 I charge you by the Lord that this epistle be read to all the holy brethren.
28 The grace of our Lord Jesus Christ be with you. Amen.

On spiritual matters, Paul now tells the brethren not to quench the Spirit and not to despise prophecy. But were also called to be ever diligent and warned to test all things and hold fast to all that is good and abstain from every form of evil. In this, the believer will be truly prepared for what lies ahead. Paul also encourages the brethren to rejoice always, to pray without ceasing, and in all things give thanks, for this is God's desire for us.

Finally, in looking at the first letter to the believers at Thessalonica, the following five points will help clarify Paul's teaching and give us a fuller understanding of the events surrounding the return of Jesus:

1. All believers have been called by Paul to be ready and remain faithful at all times in preparation for the return of Jesus.

2. Paul states that when Jesus returns, the dead in Christ will first rise and then those believers

who are alive at His coming will rise up to meet with Him in the air. This being known as the rapture of the saints.

3. In this first letter to the believers at Thessalonica, no specific time has been set for the Rapture of the Saints but when it happens, it will be completely unexpected and this also suggests a pre-Tribulation rapture.

4. Although there will be severe periods of persecution around the world, thankfully the saints of God will not suffer the day of God's wrath.

Today with the continued breakdown of society the world is experiencing more and more wars and hearing of rumours of war; it is therefore essential for our own safety and sense of well-being to experience the true peace of God within our lives and within the sanctuary of the family of God as we wait and prepare for Jesus return.

THE SECOND LETTER TO THE BELIEVERS AT THESSALONICA

Summary of 2 Thessalonians 1:1-12

Paul now writes a second time to the believers at Thessalonica. The believers have continued to face very troubled times and times of increased persecution and suffering. Paul encourages the brethren by stating they will be counted worthy and their troubles will soon come to an end when they see Jesus return with His mighty angels.

Paul proceeds to tell the believers that He will continue to pray for them to fulfil all the good pleasure of God's goodness and the work of faith with power. In so doing Messiah Jesus would be glorified in them.

In verse ten Paul states that with the return of Jesus the believers will not only stand in awe worshipping the returning King, but Jesus Himself will respond by coming into the midst of His people, rejoicing in the faithful ones and delighting in being able to stand with them. It is very clear that Paul believes in a literal return of Jesus and Jesus will return by placing his feet firmly upon the land where He once walked.

The Second Letter to the Believers at Thessalonica
Chapter 2
Paul's revelation of the last days comes from the very heart of God to bring comfort to the saints. Today, this revelation gives hope to believer, especially when the fear of the future grips so many.

2 Thessalonians Chapter 2 verses 1 to 8

In the first eight verses of chapter two, Paul addresses five issues that relate directly to Jesus return.

1. The Rapture of the Saints.
2. The Day of Judgement.
3. The Falling Away.
4. The Revealing of the Man of Sin.
5. The Works of the Restrainer.

1. The Rapture of the Saints

2 Th 2:1 -2 Now, brethren, concerning the coming of our Lord Jesus Christ and our gathering together to Him.

Although the timing of the Rapture of the Saints is an important issue, to argue about its timing can be extremely destructive. Jesus and Jesus only must be at the centre of any study of the prophetic word and not the Rapture or Antichrist or the Mark of the Beast or any other factor.

I would also like to reiterate what Jesus told His disciples, that only His heavenly Father knows when His Son will return, no one not even Jesus knows when that time will be. These words of Paul should not be ignored, and any attempt to discover the specific date of the return of Jesus is contrary to the warnings of scripture.

THE DISAPPEARANCE OF THE SAINTS AND THE NEW AGE PRESS

I have also been aware of a variety of reports within New Age publications relating to a future disappearance of a large section of the earth's population. Thus providing an alternative reason for the future disappearing of the Saints of God from off the face of the planet.

Many within the New Age movement believe those folk who will be removed from the earth will have been annihilated or transported to another planet for reeducation. They say this will happen because they are resisting the Age of Aquarius when all minds will be blended into one, and those who object to their minds being blended together will be resisting the shift in human consciousness that will come about as we enter into this New Age of Aquarius.

It is also believed that those who disappear during this Age will have been removed from the planet by Gaia the so-called Earth Goddess, I think it is pretty obvious where this reasoning originates.

2. The Day of Judgement

2 Thess 2:2
not to be soon shaken in mind or trouble either by spirit or by word or by letter, as if from us, as though the day of Christ had come.

At the time when Paul wrote to the believers at Thessalonica they has been told that they were now living in the day of the Wrath of God. The believers were terrified; they thought the great and terrible day of the Lord had already come upon them and so had missed the Rapture. From 2 Thessalonians 2:3, Paul proceeds to warn the believers not to let any person deceive them, for the Day of the Judgment of God had not yet come.

Within the letter to the believers at Thessalonica, Paul uses the phrase, the day of Christ or the day of the Lord. This phrase is often taken to be a reference to the specific return of Jesus, but the day of Christ or the day of the Lord has a broader meaning. According to Vines Expository Dictionary of New Testament Words, this term is a reference to the overall time of God's judgement at the end of the age.

In the Old Testament, the 'Day of the Lord' is a reference to the day of judgement that will come upon the enemies of Israel and if Israel were to sin, a time of darkness and judgement would come upon the nation of Israel. Another phrase related to the 'Day of the Lord' is the phrase 'in that Day', which is also very much associated with the final days of judgement. I have therefore listed below some examples of the use of the phrase, 'In the Day of...' located in both the Old and New Testaments.

3. The Turning Away (Apostasis)

> *2 Th 2:3*
> *Let no one deceive you by any means; for the Day will not come unless the falling away (apostasia) comes first, and the man of sin is revealed the son of perdition.*

Apostasia: (from the Greek) 'defection or revolt' - falling away - from the root 'aphistemi'.

Aphistemi: to withdraw oneself, desert a station in life, remove, absent oneself from - going away - to go away - to depart.

Most modern translations of the bible render the word Apostasia as 'turning away' with the footnote of the Amplified bible which states: "A possible rendering of the Greek apostasis is the departure [of the church]".

Paul now reminds the believers that this Apostasia, this turning away must take place before the Man of Sin is revealed. And on the revealing of the Man of Sin, he will be raised up to oppose God and even dare to sit as God, showing himself to be God. And when all is said and done God's final judgement will fall upon the earth.

4. The Man of Sin

> *2 Thess 2:3*
> *Let no one deceive you by any means for the Day will not come unless the falling away comes first and the man of sin is revealed, the son of perdition*
>
> *2 Thess 2:4*
> *Who opposes and exalts himself above all that is called God or that is worshipped, so that he sits as God in the temple of God, showing himself that he is God.*

The identity of this Man of Sin, this Son of Perdition is none other than Antichrist, the Beast of the Book of Revelation. This is the man who will draw Israel into union with the European State of Nations, currently known as the European Union and who will eventually attempt to take dominion of the world.

Standing closely behind this Man of Sin is the great adversary, Satan, whose time left on earth is very short and all he can do is roar and run around looking for whom he can devour. Satan will use this Man of

Sin for His own ends until the Lord comes in power to put an end to evil on the earth.

5. The Restrainer

2 Thess 2:5
Do you not remember that when I was still with you I told you these things?

2 Thess 2:6
And now you know what is restraining that he may be revealed in his own time.

2 Thess 2:7
For the mystery of lawlessness is already at wok only He who now restrains will do so until He is taken out of the way.

2 Thess 2:8
And then the lawless one will be revealed whom the Lord will consume with the breath of His mouth and destroy with the brightness of His coming.

We now come across a strange but important aspect of the End Times, that of the Restrainer and what he restrains. For many who have sought to discover the identity of this Restrainer there has been a tendency to ignore what is being restrained. Once again a clue to the identity of both the Restrainer and what is being restrained are stated in the text. According to verse 7 lawlessness will be restrained until the Restrainer is removed out of the way.

Who is the Restrainer and what is being restrained?

KATECHO: Restrain, Restrainer, Restraining, Restraineth - To hold fast or down - to be restrained in development.

The Greek word Katecho not only suggests a person or animal being restrained but also a process of restraint. This process of restraint can take many forms, a clear example of this would be that of a valve or tap restricting a flow of water. That is, a restraining process already at work and which is able to control, check, repress, hold back, limit.

In this Chapter, the restraint is referred to in a social context, *"For the mystery of lawlessness is already at work; only He who now restrains will do so until He is out of the way.*

According to Paul this lawlessness was somewhat of a mystery and yet is already at work in peoples' lives and in society as a whole. The full extent of this lawlessness will only come to a climax when the Restrainer or restraining influence is removed from the earth.

Lawlessness not only suggests an increase in crime, but also suggests a complete breakdown of society with many people taking the law into their own hands. This Lawlessness is at the heart of any anarchist or Lawless state. If this type of society were to be actively promoted by government, woe betide the citizens of that country.

Now imagine the complete removal of all laws and social constraints from society with every individual living according to their own conscience or lack of, then we will begin to understand the work of the enemy during the time of the end.

Now consider Lawlessness on a global scale.

Evil has always been present within society, but today we see evil being perpetrated across the globe on an unprecedented scale. The full extent of Lawlessness has not yet been released across the face of the earth. However, we have had a taste of what is to come.

Along with the continual destabilisation of society the present increase in lawlessness will continue and according to verse 8, when the Restrainer is removed, lawlessness will be completely unrestrained and complete anarchy will be brought upon the earth.

In Great Britain and the US today, we see the first fruits of this Lawless state; people living without any concern or regard for tomorrow or for the sanctity of life, for today we truly live in an "eat, drink and be merry for tomorrow we die" society, and tomorrow's troubles will only grow worse.

Paradoxically, when the completely Lawless Society arrives in all its fullness, Antichrist will be required to apply draconian measures to keep control of the world's population. Today, the system for the control of this type of state is now being put in place, with the first stage of this process is that of continually monitoring every individual's movements.

Furthermore, the lack of the sanctity of life seen around the world will pale into insignificance when

Antichrist comes to power.

Who or what is the Restrainer? And what restrains the Man of Sin from committing his ultimate crime?

Great debate has taken place concerning the identity of the Restrainer. Traditionally there have been three main contenders for this position:-

i.   Human government controlled by the Lawless One.

ii   The Holy Spirit as Restrainer.

iii   The Ekklesia or Church as Restrainer.

I. Human Government controlled by the Lawless One

There are a number of Christians who believe the Man of Sin himself is the Restrainer and that he restrains himself and will only be revealed at a time of his own choosing. Then, at the time of the end, Antichrist will unleash this great weapon "Lawlessness" upon the face of the earth.

This suggestion misrepresents the above passage because Satan is kept in check only by the hand of God and what God has put in place to restrain him.

ii. God's Holy Spirit

God's Holy Spirit has generally been considered as the Restrainer of Lawlessness. It has been suggested that when Holy Spirit is removed from off the earth at the end of the age, Lawlessness will be given free rein to carry out its works, yet we know that during this time God's Holy Spirit will continue to be at work on earth and will continue to convict of Sin.

Throughout the Book of Revelation we also read of those believers who are alive during the time of Tribulation.   Will God's Holy Spirit not be working in the lives of these believers and will He not be the source of their power?

The power of God's Holy Spirit is manifest in a number of different ways upon the earth and will so continue even during the time of Tribulation.

Although the presence of God will be greatly diminished during this coming time, God's Holy Spirit will still be present to convict of sin and empower believers in their witness of God.

iii. THE EKKLESIA OR CHURCH AS RESTRAINER

Once again, I have chosen to use the term Ekklesia to define the true body of believers rather than use the term, Church.   The term Church implies many different meanings to many different people.   The term Ekklesia conforms to the original Greek meaning of the description of the true body of believers.

According to Jesus, one function of the Ekklesia or gathering of believers, as well as an individual believer, is to act as a restraining force to resist the influence of evil across the world, to strengthen the saints and encourage them to be salt and light.

Mat 16:13-18
13 When Jesus came into the region of Caesarea Philippi, He asked His disciples, saying, "Who do men say that I, the Son of Man, am?"
14 So they said, "Some say John the Baptist, some Elijah, and others Jeremiah or one of the prophets."
15 He said to them, "But who do you say that I am?"
16 Simon Peter answered and said, "You are the Christ, the Son of the living God."
17 Jesus answered and said to him, "Blessed are you, Simon Bar-Jonah, for flesh and blood has not revealed this to you, but My Father who is in heaven.
18 And I also say to you that you are Peter, and on this rock I will build My church, and the gates of Hades shall not prevail against it.

With reference to the above passage, there was to be an unceasing battle between the Ekklesia of God and the gates of Hades, (or Hell). Therefore, since the time of Jesus there has been an ongoing battle between the gates of hell and against the true Church, and thankfully this battle has already been won.

The Church as the Restrainer

If the Ekklesia of God acts as the Restrainer and then, at a certain time, is removed from the earth, Antichrist will only be free to rise to the fullness of power that God will allow, and woe unto the earth during this time.

2 Th 2:9-11
9 The coming of the lawless one is according to the working of Satan, with all power, signs, and lying wonders,
10 and with all unrighteous deception among those who perish, because they did not receive the love of the truth, that they might be saved.
11 And for this reason God will send them strong delusion, that they should believe the lie,

Our Heavenly Father is slow to anger and quick to save, but believers can be sure of this one thing, God's anger will be poured out upon all evil and the world as it gives itself over to Satan.

2 Th 2:12-17
12 that they all may be condemned who did not believe the truth but had pleasure in unrighteousness.
13 But we are bound to give thanks to God always for you, brethren beloved by the Lord, because God from the beginning chose you for salvation through sanctification by the Spirit and belief in the truth,
14 to which He called you by our gospel, for the obtaining of the glory of our Lord Jesus Christ.
15 Therefore, brethren, stand fast and hold the traditions which you were taught, whether by word or our epistle.
16 Now may our Lord Jesus Christ Himself, and our God and Father, who has loved us and given us everlasting consolation and good hope by grace,
17 comfort your hearts and establish you in every good word and work.

When the true Ekklesia of God is removed from earth to meet with Jesus in the air, Antichrist will then be revealed to the world and the world will be thoroughly deceived.

What Can Be Expected as the Return of Jesus Draws Ever Closer?

As the dark clouds of the Second World War approached the warning signs were ignored. The warning signs of this next time of trouble must not be brushed aside. Today, with the dark clouds once again forming; laws changing, politics and business developing in ways unheard of even twenty years ago, we are entering a very troubled time.

On a biological front Genetic biologists striving to create life, Medical Science striving to extend life and weapons manufacturers striving to destroy life. And with the influence of the Internet we are now seeing the growth of one common language. Was this not God's concern with Babel, one common language? "then nothing would be beyond the ability of the human race."

Today's internet is only a precursor of what is to come; the present world-wide communications systems will eventually allow world politics to be totally controlled by one world dictator. A New World Order under the dominion of Antichrist will eventually attempt to take control of the world's political system and his system of political management will be totally devoid of God and totally opposed to the ways of God.

During the time ahead there will also continue to be a polarisation of society of those who accept the new way and those people who oppose. People who make a stand against evil will pay with their very lives. There will be other groups of people who are not believers and who for their own reasons object to the changes in society, these folk must be prayed for, that they too will see the truth of the Gospel and turn to Jesus before it is too late.

Throughout the time of the seven-year reign of Antichrist there will be no such thing as organised Christianity, for there will be no formal Church. True faith will be totally repressed and the only expression of this faith will be in the form of small cells and groups of friends who truly trust each other and who will be living for the Gospel at the expense of their very own lives.

It is our preparation at this present time that will, at a future date, help provide the Tribulation Saints with the much needed resources that they will need as they spread the Word of God and fight for the Gospel of Christ with their very lives. The testimony of Corrie Ten Boom is prophetic of what may be ahead for these true saints of God during the last of the very last days.

Chapter 3

In this final chapter of Paul's second letter to the believers at Thessalonica, Paul's passion for his calling and for the community of believers is once again clearly evident. Paul gave up all to follow his Master and he calls us to do the same. Paul's desire is that God's word would run swiftly and be glorified, and

God's family would be delivered from unreasonable and wicked men who hindered the way of faith.

Today, as we see the return of Jesus coming ever closer, Paul reminds us of the faithfulness of our Lord, that it is He who establishes us and guards us from the evil one. With a God like this, who can be against us and therefore, whom do we fear?

We can take confidence knowing that the Lord will direct our hearts in the love of God and in the fellowship of His Holy Spirit.

 Paul now warns believers to avoid every brother who walks disorderly, who is a busybody and who deviates from his teaching. This is especially relevant at this time as the enemy is running around attempting to deceive and devour those whom he may.

As we continue to look to Jesus, we can be assured that He will keep us all from the evil one and Jesus will present us holy and blameless before our heavenly Father. Paul also reminds us not to be a burden on others and he sets himself up as an example, encouraging us to work diligently supporting ourselves as we work.

As the return of Jesus draws ever closer, it is vital to listen to Paul's desire and the blessing he places upon every true believer, "May the Lord of peace Himself give you peace always in every way and his desire is that the grace of our Lord Jesus Christ be with us all."

With encouragement such as this, whom shall we fear?

This time should be a time of great rejoicing as we prepare for the coming of our Lord and Master, Messiah Jesus.